P9-CCH-833

# It's Up To Us

by
**John Graham**

for
The Giraffe Heroes Program

with a foreword by
Patch Adams

Stick Your Neck Out

*The Giraffe Project*

Published by
The Giraffe Project
PO Box 759
Langley WA 98260

©1999 the Giraffe Project

All rights reserved

First printing 1999

No part of this book may be reproduced in any form, or by any electronic, mechanical or other means, without permission in writing from the publisher.

Manufactured in the United States of America

Copyediting: A.T. Birmingham-Young and Kate Wright
Cover and page designs: Ann Medlock
Production management: Karyn Watkins
Illustrator: Art Bouthillier

The Summer Day from *House of Light* by Mary Oliver
© 1990 by Mary Oliver
Reprinted by permission of Beacon Press, Boston

*Library of Congress Catalog Card Number* - 99-97193

Graham, John, 1942—
It's Up To Us
by John Graham

ISBN 1-893805-00-X

Printed on recycled paper

### *Nobis est*—It's up to us

That's the motto of the Giraffe Project.
The idea is that nobody's going to magically appear and make everything better in
our lives. So we don't wait around, whining
and wondering why "they" don't make it
all the way it should be. Instead, we stick
our necks out and move into courageous,
caring action ourselves.

# ACKNOWLEDGEMENTS

This book was created with the intense and noisy collaboration of many talented people who care deeply about young people and the challenges they face.

Ann Medlock has been most responsible for helping shape the book's content, style and tone. She was the ringleader of a team that met weekly around the big red table in our office, discussing drafts and finding more good reasons than I care to admit for sending me back to my keyboard. Their biggest challenge was to get me to lighten up; they were relentless and, I hope, successful. The team members were A.T. Birmingham-Young, Jennifer Sand, Karyn Watkins, Kate Wright and the two teens on staff, Tyler Thompson and Kate Watson. Hallie Larsen contributed to early drafts before she left for college.

The stories of Giraffes were originally written by a number of people, most notably Lynn Willeford and Ann Medlock, who also designed the cover and the pages, working with Production Manager Karyn Watkins who mastered innumerable cranky software programs to produce one fine looking book. Tyler Thompson and Malory Graham did the Resource section. Our cartoonist was Art Bouthillier; copy editors A.T. Birmingham-Young and Kate Wright; printer Emerald City Graphics.

We got invaluable feedback on early drafts from teachers and youth program directors including Judy Thorslund, Jean Shaw, Dee Dickinson and Vivian Ashmawi.

All curriculum work at the Giraffe Project draws on the wisdom of our Advisory Board, which includes Peggy Charren, David Elkind, Alfie Kohn, Thomas Lickona, Kate McPherson, Michael Rothenberg MD, and Dee Dickinson of New Horizons for Learning and the Giraffe Project Board of Directors.

Our work on this book was made possible by development funds provided by the Henry M. Jackson Foundation, the Educational Foundation of America, Nancy S. Nordhoff, and the hundreds of generous individuals who support the work of the Giraffe Project.—JG

# CONTENTS

# FOREWORD

All the way back in 1984, Patch Adams, MD, was named a Giraffe by the Giraffe Project, the nonprofit that publishes this book. Giraffes stick their necks out for the common good, and Patch was certainly doing that. As medical care becomes more and more costly, this physician decided to make money the least important factor in the health equation. Patch wouldn't take money from the patients who came to his Gesundheit clinic, and he wouldn't take any from their insurance companies. To pay the clinic's bills, he worked night shifts at a mental hospital.

A public television documentary about the Giraffe Project introduced him to millions of people across the country as the doctor in a clown suit who said he was "throwing a pie in the face" of expensive, depersonalized medical care. Now the whole world knows Patch, even if they think he looks like Robin Williams.

These days, when people ask him for autographs, they get a present—a tiny flyer called "Take 10 and Call Me in the Morning." In it Patch prescribes 10 books, 10 web sites, 10 questions, 10 ideas, 10 magazines and 10 things to do. We can't give you the whole flyer here, but some excerpts fit especially well with what this book has to say. One of the questions: "If compassion and generosity were the measure of success that money and power are now, how would your life change?" And some things to do: "Turn off your TV and become interesting." "Take your vacations in your own home town and spend the money working on projects there that help build community." (You can pick up more wisdom from Patch at www.patchadams.org.)

Knowing that he shared our view that people are, at heart, brave and compassionate, I asked Patch if he had anything he'd like to say to high school students. He said "Yes and Yahoo!" and sent the following message for you.—the Editor

The human world needs major shifts in activity if human culture is to survive. No longer can we wait until "Tomorrow." But the world society's lust for money and power has left much of the population feeling powerless to affect change. Consumerism has put value in things and power and has left people feeling depressed, anxious—and bored. Young people who see adults in this condition experience a crisis in meaning.

John Graham's book is the golden ticket to meaning. He's giving you the ABC's of making your life count. Bless you, John.

I know how to make a project happen, even if in our case it will take 33 years.:-} I've had to learn through relentless trial and error. I wish I had had John's book! It doesn't tell you the task will be easy to do, but it tells you how to do important, complicated, difficult things without making every mistake I made.

No longer does a young brave (I like the word "brave") have to go into the woods with a piece of flint and a knife and come back days later with a vision and a plan. You can just read It's Up To Us, a comprehensive, programmed text, with many fun, important exercises that will make your quest—whatever it is—intelligent, creative and enriching.

We who want a world of peace and justice know it can come if each of us envisions our role and then does it. And I'm sure we must not make social change a long, arduous, lonely, sacrificing journey. It is the task of social change artists to find humongous fun and delight at every turn, to feel that each day good things happen as a consequence of their joyful effort.

The sweet nectar of the quest, (here you can burst into a rousing rendition of "To Dream the Impossible Dream") is the fuel for sustained effort. If we radiate our joy in the effort then, like Tom Sawyer, we get all the other kids involved, not out of duty but for the thrill of involvement—and John provides the play book for the action.

In the world of computer games, players become fully absorbed in a few variables that they master to progress to ever higher, more complicated variables. The higher the progress, the more exhilarated the player. This hunger for exhilaration leads to the creation of ever more complicated games. There are magazines that function as primers, helping a person learn and master the games quicker. All this for a goal that has no meaning.

John Graham has made a primer for the most complicated of games—social change. One of the raw thrills of being a change agent is being engrossed in a game with many more variables than all the computer games put together. Do you dare to master this game?

Everything I read in these pages made me smile and shake my head in agreement as something I learned along the way. This is not an academic, rhetorical, hypothetical treatise on making a difference. This is a guide book. I can't wait for them to be on the bookshelves so I can hand them out.

May all who open this book feel they have drawn Excalibur from the stone, and may they use that surge of empowerment to join all those who stick their necks out for a better world. I'll meet you Out There.

(In peace ☆ Patch)

Patch with friend.

*Tell me, what is it you plan to do*

*with your one wild and precious life?*

—Mary Oliver

CHAPTER ONE

# Living a Meaningful Life

L ook around you. Look at everyone you know and ask yourself—*Are they leading meaningful lives?*

What kind of question is that?

It may be the most important one you can ask because it's got everything to do with what you want for your own life.

Just about everybody wants a life that's meaningful—whether
we're sixteen or 106. We want to be able to look at ourselves in the
mirror and know that who we are and what we're doing *matters*,
that we're not just marking time. We want to feel a purpose for our
lives that fulfills our yearning for meaning, and makes us feel totally
alive.

But I'm guessing that, as you look around, you won't see a lot of
people who feel this kind of fulfillment. There's a lot that can get in
the way.

One thing that can get in the way is *stuff*. You're living in a culture that would like you to believe that your true worth is in what
you buy. All around you, every day, there are messages that your
life will be perfect if you have this cool car, that knock-em-dead
shirt, the right music—always something you have to buy. But
when's the last time something you bought made your life mean-

ingful, or even made you feel good for very long? Still, for a lot of people the game goes on—they buy more stuff, still looking for the happiness fix the ads promise. And it *is* a fix, with all the addictive qualities of momentary pleasure followed by a letdown, followed by an elevated need that can never be satisfied.

When you watch television or go to the mall, you see ads designed to sell stuff to people your age. You and I both know that the companies that create those messages are focused on one thing—getting you to buy products. To get you to do that, they've developed clear ideas about who you are. What are their pictures of you? Are they right?

◆••••••••••••••••••••••••••••••••••••••••••••••••••••••••••••◆

Chasing *stuff* is just one way to miss having a meaningful life. Look at all the people around you who are chasing status and power, always headed up some ladder. This game can go on forever too. People struggle to get to the next rung, and when they get there, what they see is the rung above that.

I know about chasing status and power. I was a Foreign Service Officer for 15 years and moved up the ladder quickly—I did key jobs for the United States at the United Nations and in NATO. The most important day of the year for me was the day when the promotion list came out. When my name was on it, I went out to celebrate, but the feeling of emptiness always came back. What I was doing wasn't fulfilling.

Even people who make it to the top can still feel empty. Take a look at people you know who have power or status. Some of them *may* lead meaningful lives, but you won't find many who will say that it's power or status that's filled their yearning for meaning. If they are truly fulfilled, it's because of something else.

## What's the point?

Chasing stuff, or status, or power,
is not the path to a meaningful life.

Then what is? Consider this story ~

When he read about the murder of a Pakistani child who had spoken out against child labor abuse in his country's carpet weaving industry, Toronto student Craig Kielburger didn't intend to start a global movement. He just knew something had to be done. He formed Free the Children, a nonprofit youth organization dedicated to the elimination of child labor and the end of exploiting children worldwide. "What this is all about is political will," explains Craig. "If our own country and other countries made it clear that child labor is both illegal and unacceptable, then this problem wouldn't exist."

The then 12-year-old set out to create that political will, embarking on a seven-week fact-finding trip through five Asian countries, attracting major media coverage along the way. Soon after, Craig presented his findings to a U.S. Congressional Policy Committee and met with the Vice President and with representatives of the International Labor Organization at the United Nations in New York. He went to Geneva, Switzerland for a World Council of Churches Meeting, where he urged the churches to take on this international problem.

Within two years, Free the Children had raised enough money to underwrite its outspoken leadership role and its two main projects: an education and rehabilitation center that takes in Pakistani youngsters who have escaped backbreaking 14-hour workdays and an informal

3

school for young children, keeping them out of the child labor system. The following year, Germany adopted a tag called "Rugmark," for carpets that were not made through the exploitation of children. A coalition of major US sporting goods manufacturers has pledged not to buy soccer balls stitched by Pakistani children.

Says Craig, "I'd like to make a difference here, and I see that what's needed to solve this problem is for everyone to get involved and relay the message that we want this to change."

As branches of Free the Children pop up all over Canada and the United States, Craig inspires his peers to claim a lead role in stopping this centuries-old horror. "We're capable of doing more than watching television, playing video games, or hanging around malls. Young people have the power to make a positive contribution to this world. I won't give up until the exploitation of all children has ended and all children have their rights."

Craig Kielburger didn't just listen to the stories of child slave labor and complain about how awful it was. He didn't wait for someone with more experience and training to "fix the problem." He stuck his neck out to take on a challenge that most adults would rather ignore. He did what he did because helping end the suffering of those children *meant* something to him.

Craig Kielburger is a Giraffe. "Giraffes" are people commended by the Giraffe Project, an organization that since 1982 has been honoring people who stick their necks out for the common good, that is, something that benefits many people. We tell the stories of "Giraffes" in the media and in schools, and they become models for others.

Giraffes are men, women and kids, and they're from many races, religions and backgrounds. They're truck drivers, students, retirees, artists, waitresses, doctors, homemakers, businesspeople and teachers. We've honored hundreds of them; some of their stories are in this book.

Giraffes are working on many different issues, from poverty to gang violence to environmental pollution. *One thing that's common to all of them is that they lead meaningful lives.* Win, lose or draw they're living fully, giving their all. They know why they get up in the morning, why they do things that may be scary and difficult but must be done if their cause is to be served.

When the Giraffe Project finds Giraffes like Craig, it gets their stories told on television, in magazines and newspapers, on the World Wide Web and in schools. Other people see or hear these stories, and are inspired to take on challenges *they* see, from combating hunger and disease, to cleaning up polluted rivers and revitalizing inner cities. The Giraffe Heroes Program brings Giraffe stories, themes and practical guidance for service projects into schools and youth organizations.

*Win, lose or draw, Giraffes are living fully.*

Giraffes lead meaningful lives. But as you noticed, a lot of other people never get there. Some of them get sidetracked by the stuff they buy and the status and power they seek. Another way to keep meaning out of your life is to pretend that meaning doesn't exist, that *nothing* is meaningful.

Granted, you're living in a tough world. It's chaotic and dangerous. It's got AIDs and everyday violence and too many people trapped in jobs they hate. So some people look at all of it and just give up, just put in time, just get by. They justify dropping out of their own lives by saying none of it matters, or, even if it does, that nothing can be done to make it better.

It makes sense—in a way. If you think everything is hopelessly messed up and that nothing you or anyone else does matters, why bother trying to accomplish anything?

But that isn't living—it's becoming a zombie, joining the living dead. Some zombies decide to drug or drink themselves out of reality, others bury themselves in work; all of them have given up on being truly alive.

---

## What's the point?

You can be fully alive by doing things
that are meaningful to you.
People who lead meaningful lives, like Giraffes,
don't find that meaning in possessions or positions;
they find it in personal commitments to goals
bigger than their own needs.

---

You don't have to find a deep commitment when you're 12, like Craig Kielburger did. You find it when you find it. But whenever you start, it's this active, personal commitment to goals bigger than you are that generates the personal enthusiasm, passion and power of a meaningful life. That's true for Giraffes. It can be true for you too.

Big goals can come in many forms—some people set out to be billionaires, or to win the Olympic 100-meter dash. What we've found at the Giraffe Project is that the only goals that provide real, lasting meaning are goals of service—of acting for the common good, doing something that benefits other people.

For Craig Kielburger, the service is stopping child slave labor. When I finally found what it was that made *my* life meaningful, it wasn't chasing stuff or status or power; it was helping end injustice and suffering in the world.

Throughout my time in the Foreign Service I'd seen oppression, hunger and war all over the world, close up. For most of my career, however, I wasn't concerned about the suffering all this caused. What really interested me was trying to outsmart other countries and gain advantages for ours—then enjoying the praise when I succeeded. The low point came at the United Nations when I finally understood that none of this was fulfilling to me. The emptiness was intolerable. Then I discovered that I could take all the skills I'd been using to play political power games and focus them instead on helping end racial oppression in South Africa and killing in Central America. Helping stop the suffering for so many people was satisfying in a way no promotion or power game had ever been. I'd found the path of service that made my life meaningful, and that discovery made all the difference—to the people I was helping, and to me. I left the Foreign Service when I saw there were opportunities for helping people close to home as well as abroad. Soon after that, I became Executive Director of the Giraffe Project.

Here are two more people who found meaning through service. Both have been honored by the Giraffe Project as Giraffes ~

As a young housewife and mother, Lois Gibbs learned that her Love Canal neighborhood in Niagara Falls NY was built on a toxic waste dump. Her children were sick, possibly fatally. She had to do something. Gibbs set out to talk to neighbors about what they could do. But she was so unsure of herself that she quit after knocking on one door. Reminding herself that people's lives were at stake, she went back out and knocked on door after door. People called her nuts, or "that hysterical housewife." "Experts" told her she didn't know what she was talking about, but she kept on, gradually convincing other people to question what was going on, and not roll over to the corporate polluters and government officials who said nothing was wrong. Eventually, the effort she started got all 900 families in Love Canal relocated.

Gibbs also went to Congress, where she made sure that what had happened at Love Canal powered a drive to create the Superfund, a multi-billion dollar Federal program that forces polluters to clean up their toxic messes.

Gibbs went on to found the Citizens' Clearinghouse for Hazardous Wastes, now called the Center for Health, Environment and Justice, which helps other toxin-plagued communities not only clean up the poisons, but also work for safe jobs, drinkable water, uncontaminated foods, recycling, and reduction and proper disposal of wastes. Only seven years after she started, the Clearinghouse had five regional offices and an active membership of over 5,000 grassroots organizations.

Lois Gibbs went from being a shy housewife, afraid to talk to her neighbors, to being a national leader on an issue of vital concern, all because keeping her family and other families safe from toxic wastes *meant* so much to her. She didn't find the meaning in her life from getting her picture in the papers—although she *did* become famous—she found her meaning in service.

Have you ever been alone against the crowd—maybe even facing active, vocal opposition—when you knew you were right? What did you do? If you kept going, why did you?

◆••••••••••••••••••••••••••••••••••••••••••••••••••••••••••◆

Here's another Giraffe story—this one about someone who never got his name on national television ~

I n the small Idaho town of Marsing, football was everything. On Friday nights, hundreds of people from the town and the farms around it would come to watch the Marsing Huskies play. Ernesto "Neto"

Villareal was a star player on the high school team, good enough to be considered for a college athletic scholarship.

The problem was the fans. When the players did something good, everyone cheered. But when they made a mistake, something else happened. If the player was Latino, like Villareal, people shouted insults like, "Stupid Mexican!" It happened a lot, and people seemed not to notice. But the Latino players noticed. Villareal led them in deciding that they wouldn't play anymore unless the insults stopped. Their coach told them they would only make things worse—the team couldn't win the state championship if they stopped playing. Villareal also knew that he could lose his chance at a football scholarship. But stopping the insults meant more than a scholarship. Villareal talked to the student body president, who then talked to the principal. When the principal refused to do anything, the other Latino players were ready to give up and resume playing. Not Villareal. He went over the principal's head to the School Board, even though he'd seen one of the School Board members shouting insults at Latino players. It was difficult, but Villareal told them why he was refusing to play. "Now," he said, "they can't say nobody told them."

The student body president, inspired by Villareal's courage, wrote a letter asking adults to stop the insults, and asking officials to throw people out of the stadium if they didn't stop. Led by Villareal, the Latino players agreed to play only if the letter was read over the loudspeaker at the game.

The principal refused to read the letter, but the school superintendent overruled him and directed that the letter be read. When it was, people in the stadium stood and applauded. And the insults stopped. Neto Villareal had scored a touchdown for tolerance. Combating racism in his town may have been the biggest win of his career.

Why didn't Neto Villareal give up when he ran into the first adult blocking his path? Hearing a few rude calls during a game couldn't have been *that* bad. Or could it? Would *you* have kept pressing the issue, as Villareal did? What would have been lost if he'd quit?

◆••••••••••••••••••••••••••••••••••••••••••••••••••••••••••◆

As with Craig Kielburger, the key to meaning for Lois Gibbs and Neto Villareal was in carrying out personal commitments to goals bigger than themselves and their own needs—goals of service. For Gibbs it's protecting people from pollution; for Villareal it was stopping racist insults.

> ## What's the point?
> Finding meaning in your life
> and serving the common good are linked.
> This book is about finding a path of service
> that brings you meaning and joy,
> and following that path with courage and skill.

It's not about being a superhero. It's about starting from where you are, using *your* talents, personality, enthusiasm and preferences. The stories about Giraffes might suggest issues you'd like to work on. But this book is not about Giraffes, it's about you.

Is there an issue out there with your name on it? Something you could do to make a difference in your school, your community and even your world? It could be working to change a climate of violence in your school, speaking up when that's hard to do, or organizing campaigns to help tackle racism or homelessness—there are hundreds of issues and problems out there.

Not for you? Well, that's what a lot of Giraffes thought too, at least in the beginning. Then they saw that the problems in front of them weren't going away and nobody else was stepping up to solve them. So they stuck their necks out, despite their own fears, despite the apathy or even the opposition of people around them. They found that committing themselves in this way gave their lives meaning. And while they were making the world a better place, they gained self-confidence and skills. *This book*

Many of them found that courageous service became *can help* the adventure of their lives. It's been that way for me. I went to sea on a freighter when I was 16, putting into ports *you* all over the Far East. Did it again when I finished high school—I was the only freshman to arrive at my college via *fine-tune* tramp steamer. As a junior, I was on a team that made the first direct ascent of the north wall of Mt. McKinley in Alaska, a climb so dangerous it's never been done again. When I *what you* graduated, I hitchhiked around the world, then joined the Foreign Service which sent me into the middle of a revolu- *already* tion in Libya, and to one of the hottest areas of the war in Vietnam. I've been shot at on three continents. I've even *know.* survived a shipwreck in the Gulf of Alaska.

*But none of these adventures match the excitement of service.* My job at the Giraffe Project takes me all over the world, helping people in organizations and communities stick their necks out to take on challenges and solve problems. It's the biggest and best adventure yet.

If you've never considered sticking your neck out for anything, the stories of Giraffes in this book may change your mind, and the coaching tips may convince you that you can develop both the courage and the skills you need to act.

If you're considering getting involved for the first time—you've just learned of a project you'd like to join, or an issue that concerns you is not being addressed and you'd like to start your own project—this book will give you the guidance you need to succeed.

If you've got some experience, then look in this book for new approaches to solving problems, and for ways of helping you fine-tune what you already know.

You can use these ideas in any area of your life, acting alone or with groups, including your family. No matter what challenge you might take on and when you might do it, the concepts and coaching tips here will raise your chances for success.

If the challenges that most concern you now are personal—maybe trying to resolve a problem at home or a conflict in a relationship—what this book has to say can help you take the right steps in these realms as well.

Some of the "how to" material here comes from Giraffes, and their stories illustrate points throughout the book. Other ideas and stories come from my own experiences. All of it is field-tested, not just untried theories.

This book is a coaching manual. All of us at the Giraffe Project hope it moves you to find and tackle a challenge in your school, your community—wherever you may be or come to be. We also hope what you learn here can guide you through a lifetime—a *meaningful* lifetime—of sticking your neck out for the common good.

✔ Just about everybody wants a life that's meaningful—to know that who we are and what we're doing *matters*, that we're not just marking time. We want to feel a purpose for our lives that fulfills us and makes us feel totally alive.

✔ Buying stuff, or gaining status or power doesn't fill that yearning for a meaningful life.

✔ Another way to make sure your life is meaningless is to decide that *nothing* is meaningful. But that isn't living—it's becoming a zombie, joining the living dead.

✔ You can choose instead to be fully and completely alive by doing things that are meaningful to you. The challenges are out there—in your school, your community, and in the world-at-large.

✔ People who lead meaningful lives find that meaning in carrying out personal commitments to goals bigger than their own needs—especially goals of service. It's that active commitment that generates their enthusiasm, passion and power. It can be the same for you. This book is about finding a path of service that brings you meaning and joy, and following that path with courage and skill.

✔ Getting actively involved in service isn't about being a superhero. It's about you starting from where you are, using *your* talents, personality, enthusiasm and skills.

✔ Sticking your neck out to help others can be the adventure of your life.

**At the Giraffe Project, we collect wise quotes.
Here are some of our favorites about meaning and service ~**

*I find that if I'm thinking too much of my own problems and the fact that at times things are not just like I want them to be, I don't make any progress at all. But if I look around and see what I can do, and go on with that, then I move on.* —Rosa Parks

*You have not lived today until you have done something for someone who can never repay you.* —John Bunyan

*The people I feel sorry for are those who quit, who give up and drop out at some point along the way . . . who shut their eyes, their ears and their minds, and settle down in sullenness and apathy . . . to live out the remainder of their lives like starfish or toads.* —Earl Nightingale

*In this world everything changes except good deeds and bad deeds; these follow you as the shadow follows the body.* —Ruth Benedict

*Technology enables us to do almost anything we can imagine, but we are gradually losing track of what is worth doing.* —Willis Harmon

*Freedom is not worth fighting for if it means no more than license for everyone to get as much as he can for himself.* —Dorothy Canfield Fisher

*This is the true joy in life, the being used for a purpose recognized by yourself as a mighty one; the being of a force of nature instead of a feverish, selfish little clod of ailments and grievances complaining that the world will not devote itself to making you happy.* —George Bernard Shaw

*No society of nations, no people within a nation, no family can benefit through mutual aid...unless we all see and act as though the other [person's] welfare determines our own welfare.* —Henry Ford

*It is not fair to ask of others what you are not willing to do yourself.* —Eleanor Roosevelt

*When you stop giving and offering something to the rest of the world, it's time to turn out the lights.* —George Burns

# CHAPTER TWO

# Start Here:
# What Would You Like to Change in Your World?

F ind a way to serve and you'll find a path to meaning. There are plenty of ways to serve, and many paths. Ask yourself what you care about. That can help you find a path of service that fits who you are and what you like to do.

We're not talking about personal things you care about like whether or not somebody likes you, or perfecting your jump shot. I mean something that's bigger than you and your own needs. Maybe it's something that's been bugging you for months. Maybe it's something you've just learned about.

If you can't think of an issue you care about, look around. What do you think could be better? Are there people in your community who don't have enough food or who have no shelter? Is there racial or religious prejudice that turns people in your community against each other? Are there too many fights in your school, too many kids abusing drugs, getting pregnant or dropping out? Is the air where you live fit to breathe and the water fit to drink? Are there global issues that concern you—environmental issues or human rights problems like the one that Craig Kielburger spotted?

Whatever the issue might be, at the Giraffe Project we say caring about an issue or a public problem means more than just wishing something good might happen, or cheering someone else on. Caring shouldn't be a spectator sport. It should mean you invest your own time, energy and resources to make a difference.

*Maybe* When you really care, you get excited about something. That feeling might not come all at once; maybe the issue has to *an issue* grow on you. This excitement will give you the energy to keep going, and help you stay committed and enthusiastic *will find* even if things get tough.

*you.* Maybe there aren't any issues you care that much about right now. OK. Just keep looking, starting from where you are. What interests you? What are you naturally good at doing? Answers to questions like these can suggest the kinds of issues you might get involved in.

You don't have to save the world—maybe the issues that grab your attention are local. Maybe they have to do with some pressing social concern and maybe they don't. Whatever they are, pay attention to them. Maybe an issue will find *you.*

The Discovery School in Coupeville, Washington is a public school for kids who've had problems with school work and discipline. When one class at the school took on The Giraffe Heroes Program, things really changed.

Intrigued by the stories of Giraffes, the kids asked themselves what issue they cared about. The choice was easy. A student had almost been hit by a car speeding past the school grounds, ignoring the speed limit to get to the nearby ferry landing. The kids knew that this wasn't the only near-miss, and if something wasn't done, somebody was going to get seriously hurt. Making the streets around their school safe was their issue.

The students started off their project by videotaping speeding cars, clocking them, and graphing the results. Then they interviewed workers in the area about near-misses these people had seen. With that data in hand, they got a State trooper to confirm their findings with his radar gun. They got one of the county commissioners to visit their school, to see the problem for himself, then made a formal presentation to all the commissioners. The result was a $12,000 traffic light, a crosswalk and the admiration of everyone who witnessed what they'd accomplished. The students themselves experienced the power of teamwork and of their own value as people who could get an important job done.

Sometimes it's easier to see an issue far away than right in front of you. Is there some local issue or problem that's affecting people you know? Something that's right in your face?

◆•••••••••••••••••••••••••••••••••••••••••••••••••••••••••◆

## Choosing an Issue

I f you're part of a group that will pick an issue and work on a service project together, it's still important for you to get clear on what *you* care about as an individual. If you've thought about what's important to you, you'll help your group make a better choice than if you just sit back and wait for others to make the decisions for you. Talk about the reasons behind your choices. Your ideas are as important as anybody else's. And speaking up may help others reflect on what's important to *them.*

If your group isn't coming up with a lot of ideas, here are some ways to get ideas flowing. They're designed for use in a group, but you can use them on your own too.

### Gimme five

Each person writes down five issues that he or she cares about in your school or community. Then five issues that are national or global. Everyone reads their choices. Someone writes all of them on a board or large sheet of paper.

### Check it out

Take a walk, singly or in groups, through your community or through other parts of your town or city. Focus on what you're seeing and sensing. How do people treat each other and their surroundings? Check out the condition of streets, buildings and open spaces. Look for safety problems, environmental pollution, etc. Then discuss as a group what you've seen. What needs to be better? What concerns you the most? What opportunities do you see for your group to make a difference? Write it all down.

### Brainstorming

You know how to do this. Everyone starts tossing out ideas for an issue the group might take on. There are no "bad" ideas. Every idea gets written down. No matter how strange an idea might sound, it could turn out to be a great one—or it can lead to someone else's great idea. The brainstorming needs to go on long enough to get everyone thinking creatively. If at some point the brainstorming session hits a lull, the process shouldn't stop. Fresh, creative ideas often appear after a lull.

*There are no bad ideas in a brainstorm.*

After you've done one—or all three—of these exercises, the group talks about all the issues that have come up, combining those that are similar. People who feel strongly about an issue can speak out for it. If there's a group consensus, fine. If not, you'll need to decide whether to take on more than one issue with the resources you've got, or just choose one.

One way to choose is to do several rounds of voting, with the lowest vote-getting idea eliminated in each succeeding round, until only one idea is left. If there are many issues to choose from, the class can eliminate the least popular two or three with each vote.

Once you've chosen the issue, the next step is to gather enough basic information about it that you have a fair picture of what you might be getting into. You need to know, for example ~

~ Who is affected by this issue—who are the "stakeholders"?

~ Has anyone else tackled this? With what results? Is anything being done now? Are there potential allies you could work with?

~ Where can you get more information on this issue if you take it on?

**Go or no go**
Given the results of your research, does this issue still seem the one to take on? If not, choose another one.

# Choosing a Project

Choosing an issue and doing some homework on it focuses your attention on what you really care about. Now it's time to sharpen that focus by creating a specific service project that addresses it. The following suggestions are written for a class or group, but you can easily adapt them if you're on your own.

**One...**
Review what you've learned so far about your issue.

> Let's say that a group decides that the issue it cares most about is pollution in their area. In gathering basic information, they find out that their local government has had a "hands-off" attitude toward polluters, even though, according to the health department, health risks are high in several areas. The group's research convinces them that local pollution is definitely the issue they want to work on.

**Two...**
Go back into brainstorming mode and toss around ideas for a specific project that addresses the issue you've chosen. What could you or your group do that would make a difference?

As part of this discussion, it's important to determine the *scope* of any service project you might create. For example, what's the maximum amount of time you've got to work on it—a whole school year, one semester...? How many hours a week could people put in?

Steer away from projects that are clearly out of reach for the time you've got, but don't settle for something that wouldn't be a stretch—cleaning up the school grounds would be way too easy. After all, this is about sticking your neck out and that means going outside your usual comfort zone.

D on't veto projects that require money, volunteers or other resources you don't now have. You can get all those things as part of the project.

Again, someone writes all the suggestions on the board, combining ideas that are similar. Anyone who feels strongly about an idea should explain why. Go for consensus, but if people can't agree, use the same voting process you used to choose the issue. It's possible for a class to break into smaller groups and do more than one project, especially if the projects are closely related, but this increases the challenges of planning and logistics. Once you've decided on a project, add as many details as you can.

*The group that picked local pollution as its issue decides to focus its project on the pollution in Lake McChubb, a ten-acre lake near the center of town. Levels of contaminants in the water have been rising for years. The health department is threatening to close the lake to swimming and fishing if the levels increase. People assume the lake will die. Trash on the shore and in the water add to the grim picture.*

*The group decides to stop the increase in contamination levels and reverse the trend. They calculate they can work on this project two Saturdays a month until school ends in June; they'll also have in-class time twice a week.*

*In doing some research, the group discovers that a major source of the pollution in Lake McChubb is household and garden chemicals like the cleaning products and weed killers used by people living near the lake. So a big part of their project will be a public information campaign about the toxic effects of these chemicals. Other details are added as the group's discussion continues. Everyone agrees that a successful project to revive the lake could help focus their community's attention on other local pollution problems, and could inspire more people to take them on.*

**Three...**
Once the project idea has been chosen, the group needs to describe it in one or two sentences, like this ~

*We'll plan and carry out a campaign to start making Lake McChubb once again a healthy, beautiful place the people of our community can enjoy and take pride in. We'll create enough momentum so the project continues on its own.*

Under this description, the group writes down whatever details it's agreed on for this project. They can add, subtract or change details as they proceed.

**Four...**

Make a poster. Give the project an interesting name—something that says what the project is and also conveys the action you'll be taking. Put the Project name across the top of the poster then write down the other information, maybe like this ~

## Scrub McChubb

*The issue—Pollution in our area*

*The project—We'll plan and carry out a campaign to start making Lake McChubb once again a healthy, beautiful place that people can enjoy and take pride in. We'll create enough momentum so the project continues on its own.*

✴ *Our project will cover the lake, the shoreline, and the residential areas within three blocks of the lake.*

✴ *We'll work every other Saturday and have two in-class sessions every week.*

✴ *We'll coordinate with city officials, local environmentalists and others, to continue to learn about the causes of the lake's pollution so that the solutions we suggest are sound.*

✴ *We'll pick up trash, replace trash cans, and remove graffiti.*

✴ *We'll organize public meetings and get media to help us spread the word on what citizens can do. We'll put up posters and create a simple brochure that we'll deliver to the homes in the area.*

✴ *We'll talk to local nurseries and hardware stores about putting warnings on house and garden products that add pollution to the lake and about suggesting alternative, less-polluting products.*

✴ *We'll create a budget, then raise the money we need for printing and supplies.*

✔ Asking what you *care* about can help you find a path of service that fits who you are and what you like to do.

✔ If you don't see an issue, look around. Look at all the things in your school, neighborhood, city and planet that could be better.

✔ Caring about an issue or a public problem has to mean more than just wishing something good might happen, or cheering for someone else. Active caring means you'll invest your own time, energy and resources to make a difference.

✔ When you really care, you feel an excitement that gives you the energy to take on the issue, and that helps you stay committed and enthusiastic even if things get tough.

✔ Maybe there aren't any issues you care that much about right now. OK. Just keep looking, starting from where *you* are.

✔ You'll help your group make a better choice of what *it* cares about if you've thought about what's important to *you*. Talk about the reasons behind your choices. Your ideas are as important as anybody else's.

✔ After you've chosen an issue, gather basic information about it so you have a picture of what you might be getting into. Whose lives are affected by this issue? Has anyone else tackled this? What were their results? Where can you go for more information if you decide to take it on?

✔ Next, sharpen your focus by creating a service project that addresses your issue. How big a project are you willing to take on? Steer away from projects that are clearly out of reach for the time you've got—but don't settle for something that won't be a stretch.

✔ Once the project has been designed, give it an interesting name and a one- or two-sentence description. Then add as many details as you can.

CHAPTER THREE

# Vision: What Would It Look Like If You Changed It?

W hen an environmental group was working to stop a big, coal-fired power plant from being built near the Grand Canyon, Michael Stewartt, a private pilot, had an idea: he and some pilot friends flew reporters and photographers over the proposed plant site, so they could see for themselves how close it was to the Canyon. It worked. Media stories forced the power company to scrap its plans.

The Grand Canyon flyover worked so well that Stewartt could "see" volunteer pilots providing the same service for other areas endangered by pollution or clearcutting. He got a wealthy Colorado rancher to share his vision of an environmental "eye-in-the-sky." The rancher let Stewartt use one of his planes and enough gas for 150 hours of flying. The new organization, "Lighthawk," was off the ground.

In the early years, Stewartt and another pilot worked primarily with conservationists in the Rocky Mountain area and with Arizona's Smelter Crisis Education Project (SCEP), laying the groundwork for a success that would really put wind

beneath Lighthawk's wings.

For 40 years, a copper smelter in Arizona had had the dubious distinction of producing more acid rain and air pollution than any other plant in the United States. When Lighthawk photographed the emissions from the smelter, helping SCEP get it shut down, conservationists realized they had a powerful new ally. Stewartt's vision of what concerned pilots like himself could do to save wilderness areas was becoming a reality. The organization grew to 30 active volunteer pilots who have their own planes and can give fast support to environmentalists.

The impact has been enormous. After a powerful politician who was a longtime timber industry advocate flew over Vancouver Island with Stewartt, she began calling for an immediate end to clearcutting. In Alaska, Lighthawk spent a week flying legislators, conservationists and reporters over the Tongass, America's largest rainforest. In the waters off the many islands and peninsulas they saw orcas, otters, dolphins and humpback whales. On land, there were grizzly bears and wolves. But in the clearcut patches where ancient old-growth Sitka spruce once stood, they saw silt-choked streams where fish could no longer live. That enlightening week helped start the ball rolling on a repeal of the Forest Service rules that allowed wholesale clearcutting in the Tongass.

Stewartt's vision grew to include flying in Southeast Asia and Costa Rica and producing television ads on the crisis in the rainforests.

## What's the point?

There are two kinds of "pictures" in this story.
One is the literal sight of pollution and clearcuts
that people get from Lighthawk airplanes.
The other is the picture Michael Stewartt "saw"
in his mind of the ways private pilots
could help stop environmental destruction—
a picture that led to Lighthawk.

S arah Swagart knew an injustice when she saw one. Swagart decided it was wrong for young skateboarders to be treated like criminals. Kids who skated in her town's parking lots and on its sidewalks were threatened with fines as high as $500, and 90 days in jail. Not a skateboarder herself, she could see that the skaters might be annoying, but they were just kids who needed a place to use their sometimes awesome skills.

A picture began to form in her mind of a legal place for the kids to skate. She formed an organization whose goal was to get the skateboarders their own place to practice—and to get the community to recognize them as athletes, not hoodlums.

Swagart shared her vision with a local architect, who volunteered to design a skateboard park. But there had to be some place to put it. Swagart realized that no matter how much it scared her to speak in public, she had to start talking if the kids were going to get some land for their park. She wrote up a petition and got signatures from kids, teachers, police officers, and even some store owners. Leading a delegation of 40 kids, she stood before the City Council and pointed out that the town had baseball fields, basketball courts, a roller rink and a swimming pool where kids could do the sports of their choice. What would be so different about a place for the skateboarders?

The biggest problem, besides the kids' bad image, was insurance liability. What if a skater got hurt and sued the city? Swagart and the skateboarders got information on safety and liability from other towns that had skateboard parks. The City Council finally agreed there could be a skateboard park next to the public swimming pool.

The vision Swagart and the skateboarders had for their park caught on. The SeaBees at a nearby Naval Air Station offered to do the construction work. Sarah's group got local businesses to donate materials. And they organized a series of events to raise money. Swagart's picture of a skaters' park is now a reality. "Before this project I'd never stand up to anybody," Swagart says. "Now, I would definitely encourage people to go for what they believe in."

## What's the point?

Sarah Swagart and Michael Stewartt
created pictures in their imaginations
of what they wanted to see happen.
These pictures motivated them and attracted support
that helped them turn the pictures into realities.

Powerful pictures like these are called "visions." *Visions are mental pictures of something that doesn't yet exist—but the pictures are so clear and strong that they help you make that something real.* Visions can help you succeed in any project or challenge, now or in the future.

People use this technique all the time. Cooks can "see" a beautiful meal on the table before they lift a spoon. Directors of plays "see" a perfect production before rehearsals begin. Free-throw shooters practice "seeing" the ball go into the basket—studies show that basketball players who spend time off the court "seeing" their shots going through the hoop improve their shooting percentages almost as much as players who actually practice with the ball.

Sometimes visions make history. When Dr. Martin Luther King, Jr. described his vision for racial justice in America in his "I Have a Dream" speech, it was unlikely that racial justice would ever become the law of the land, so strong was the opposition. But by describing a vivid picture of an America in which racial prejudice was gone, Dr. King touched millions of people's hearts and set in motion political activity throughout the country that resulted in laws that support the racial justice he could "see" coming into existence.

 Have you ever created a picture in your imagination of something that didn't exist? Maybe it was a picture of winning a close ball game, finishing a complicated project, or aceing an exam. Did you hold that picture and move toward making it happen? If you've ever done that, what was your picture? What happened?

# Putting Vision to Work

As you saw in the stories of Michael Stewartt, Sarah Swagart and Dr. King, visions aren't idle dreams or hopes or wishes; they're pictures of the intended results of *real* plans and *real* efforts.

Speaking of real plans and efforts—in the last chapter, you chose an issue you care about, did some research and created a project. Now comes a crucial step—creating your vision for your project, a detailed picture of the results you want. Why take the time? Why is this so important? A quick and silly way to remember the answer is—"IGG."

### I for inspiration

As in Dr. King's case, a powerful vision inspires people to commit, to act, to persist and to give their best.

### G for guide

A vision is a practical guide for setting goals and objectives, making decisions, and coordinating the work on any project, large or small. A vision is like "true north" on the compass; by keeping his eye on his vision for Lighthawk, Michael Stewartt kept his project on course. No matter what decisions on a project need to be made, you can test each option by asking if it will help make the vision for the project real. If the answer is "No," then don't do it.

### G for glue

A vision is glue. In a group made up of many different kinds of people, a vision can help keep everyone together for the long haul, even people who might not be used to working together in groups. If people share a vision, it's easier for them to see connections between what they want as individuals and the goals of the entire group. Sarah Swagart had to get some pretty opinionated people to work together to make the skateboard park a reality, and she couldn't have done it without getting them to share her vision.

Not every picture is a vision. Some special qualities are needed.

**To work, a vision must ~**

~ **be clear and concrete enough that you can see the details —and hear, smell and taste them!** If your vision is of creating a fantastic meal for a family event, how does the table look? How does each dish smell and taste? What do people say as they taste each dish? Is your vision achieving a personal best in sports, maybe as a runner? OK, feel the air rushing past your ears and hear people's voices urging you on. Look at the coach's stopwatch and see that you've done your best time ever.

~ **include changes in people's attitudes.** Often what's behind problems in communities are negative attitudes such as apathy and hopelessness. It's these attitudes that will cause the original problems to reappear, sooner or later, if your project doesn't address them too.

*The vision for the Lake McChubb group needs to go beyond how the lake looks when their project's finished. The lake can't be healthy and beautiful for the long-term unless the people who live around it change their attitudes toward using toxic house and garden chemicals and everyone is more mindful of not throwing trash. The Lake McChubb Group needs to "see" these attitude changes in their vision.*

~ **come from imagination, not logic.** To create a vision that's exciting and compelling, you've got to use your imagination to see and feel what does not yet exist.

Being logical is important in any project; it's a question of timing. Once you have a vision, *then* use your rational thinking skills to plan and problem-solve and take the actions that will make the vision real.

*Cleaning up Lake McChubb will require good research, intense thinking and a lot of work. But for the group that's taking this project on, success depends on first using their imaginations to create a powerful vision of people enjoying a healthy and beautiful lake.*

# How to Create a Vision

This process works for groups and it works for people who are acting on their own. Use it to create a personal vision of a significant success in your studies, in sports or at home—as well as for doing service projects. For teams and classes, there's a special synergy generated when all the members share the same vision of what they'll achieve.

Start by reviewing the poster for your project you created in the last chapter. Now imagine that you're in the future, at a date just after your project is finished. Everyone in your group needs to "see" clearly what's going on at that future date. For the Lake McChubb group that might be:

> They're all on the lake shore on a hot afternoon next June, after their project is finished. What do they see, hear, smell? How's the water? What are people doing? What are people saying to each other about the lake? The group lets the pictures come forth, drawing them or describing them in words as they emerge. Some team members see people swimming in the lake and fishing from rowboats. Others see people tossing frisbees and playing volleyball on a clean lakeshore. One guy even smells hotdogs cooking on a grill...

A useful technique here is for a group to split up into pairs and have the partners describe the scene to each other. Both of you need to speak in the present tense, not future tense—you're *in* the future looking back, with your project accomplished.

> Part of the vision for the Lake McChubb project is, "People <u>are</u> swimming and fishing..." not, "people <u>will be</u> swimming and fishing..."

If you find it hard to get a vision going, let one person pretend to be listening to the radio on that day in the future, while the other person "broadcasts" from the scene, describing what's going on, how things look, etc. to people who can't see what she sees.

As your group gets rolling, here's a technique that will add clarity to your vision: still speaking as if the project is finished, think of some obstacles you've had to overcome to succeed with your project, and then describe how you overcame them and the success that resulted. Don't stop to analyze or ponder here—just let the pictures flow. You'll be surprised at how many good problem-solving ideas appear. When you move on to actually planning and carrying out your project, this technique will help you see obstacles not as insurmountable, but as similar to the hurdles you've already jumped in your vision exercise; you've already anticipated some obstacles and how to solve them so the exercise can be a great confidence-builder for the job ahead.

When you finish talking, write down the obstacles you saw and the solutions you came up with, and put them where you can find them later. You'll use them when you do detailed planning in Chapter Six.

> Someone in the Lake McChubb group might describe obstacles overcome this way: "We thought that some people would resist the idea of giving up toxic house and garden chemicals. So we created a great brochure on good alternatives and gave them to people all over the area. We put up posters. We did interviews on radio and television and lots of people listened and watched. As more and more people started to support our idea, they talked to their neighbors, and the idea spread."

Quickly capture the pictures all the members of your group see of the completed project, taking notes while the pictures are fresh, even if that gives you just a lot of phrases. Good writing isn't the goal here. Then the group or a smaller team summarizes all the notes into one "Vision Statement" and puts it on a new poster. If there are artists in the group, they can add drawings or collages that help depict the vision. Here's the summarized Vision Statement the Lake McChubb group puts on its poster ~

> The levels of contaminants in the lake are dropping significantly. People are using the cleaner lake with confidence again—people are swimming and fishing, seniors are sitting on benches and talking, parents are tending babies and playing with older kids… Nobody in the area is using toxic chemicals—everybody is taking responsibility for keeping the lake and the lakeshore clean. People from other parts of the city are coming by and talking about cleaning up pollution problems where they live.

Did the process of creating the vision spark any new thinking about your project? Is there anything that should be added to the first poster you made, the one describing your project?

·········································

*In the process of creating their vision, the Lake McChubb group saw themselves working side by side with the people who lived around the lake, not doing all the work on their own. They realized that involving residents in this way would encourage them to take responsibility for keeping the lake clean and healthy after their project is over. So the group decides to add a sentence to their poster describing the project: "We'll work with local residents to get the job done."*

---

## What's the point?

Anyone can create a vision.
A strong vision will consistently raise the odds
of your success on any kind of project.
In my years of helping organizations, groups
and individuals solve tough problems,
I've never discovered a more powerful tool.

---

✔ Visions are clear, concrete pictures of something you'd like to happen but which doesn't yet exist. Visions are tools that can help you succeed in any kind of project or challenge, now or in the future.

✔ A vision is ~
- ~ Inspiration. A powerful vision inspires people to commit, to act, to persist, and to give their best.
- ~ Guidance for setting goals and objectives, making decisions, and coordinating the work on any kind of project, large or small.
- ~ Glue. In a group made up of many different kinds of people, a vision can help keep everyone together for the long haul.

✔ Visions aren't idle dreams or hopes or wishes—they're pictures of the intended results of real plans and real efforts.

✔ To succeed, a vision needs to ~
- ~ be so clear and concrete you can see, hear, smell and taste the details.
- ~ include changes in people's attitudes.
- ~ come from imagination, not logic.

✔ Anyone can create a vision.

**And a few wise words about dreams and visions,
from the Giraffe Project's treasury of quotes ~**

*If others can see it as I have seen it, then it may be called a vision rather
than a dream.* —Arturo Toscanini

*Hold fast to dreams/For if dreams die/Life is a broken-winged bird/
That cannot fly.* —Langston Hughes

*'Realistic people' who pursue 'practical aims' are rarely as realistic and
practical, in the long run of life, as the dreamers who pursue only their
dreams.* —Hans Selye

*We should all be concerned about the future because we will have to spend
the rest of our lives there.* —Charles Kettering

*With the supermarket as our temple and the singing commercial as our
litany, are we likely to fire the world with an irresistible vision of America's exalted purposes and inspiring way of life?* —Adlai Stevenson

*Dare to live the life you have dreamed for yourself. Go forward and make
your dreams come true.* —Ralph Waldo Emerson

*Most of the things worth doing in the world had been declared impossible
before they were done.* —Louis Brandeis

*It's kind of fun to do the impossible.* —Walt Disney

CHAPTER FOUR

# Putting Your Compassion into Action

An important part of the path to a meaningful life is *active compassion* for the people you meet on the way. "Compassion" means to care, to empathize deeply with other people, to put yourself in their shoes. "Active" means with real deeds, not just words. Here are two examples ~

Grandma Edie Lewis started rehabilitating "throwaway" kids when she found a big teenager sleeping in her snowy yard in Alaska back in the '70s. When his parents said, "You got him. You keep him," Lewis did. Soon she was running an unofficial shelter for as many as 16 "outcast" 18- to 24-year-olds.

The six-foot Alaskan businesswoman used a big chunk of her income to support "her kids." After she married, she and her husband kept up the work. When they moved to Garland, Texas they bought the perfect house—near shopping centers for jobs, a bus line for transportation, and a community college for

*Grandma Edie (left) with some of her "kids"*

training. They kept that house filled with kids other people had labeled "hopeless."

Lewis made sure they got off drugs, off booze and off the street. She made sure they got jobs, earned high school equivalency certificates and went on to community college. How did she work this magic? "Kindness kills them," she told the Giraffe Project. "The worse they are, the nicer I am to them ..."

Grandma Edie's only set rule was that people who were drunk or stoned couldn't enter the house until they sobered up. She didn't want rules so tough she had to throw kids out before they had the time to improve; that was the main reason she didn't look for government funds, which usually limited treatment time to 90 days. "They seldom come in holy terrors and leave three months later holy angels. Only God can do such miracles, and I'm not God."

Most of the holy terrors were angry, and the house took a lot of damage when they raged. One hard case had punched nine holes in the walls. After the ninth, Lewis calmly walked over and punched a hole next to it. "It made him think, 'That's not so macho, the old woman can do it,' and he never punched a hole in the wall again."

After more than two decades of caring for kids, Grandma Edie Lewis was killed in the fall of 1998 when her van was hit by a truck. A few years before she died, Lewis told us she'd been able to reach all but three of the hundreds of "incorrigibles" who had lived with her—quite a lifetime batting average.

Grandma Edie's active compassion turned kids' lives around. It moved her into the service that made her life meaningful. The same is true for this Giraffe ~

When Steve Mariotti got mugged by teenagers on a New York City street, he didn't start agitating for better police protection. Instead he started thinking of better ways that kids like the muggers could make money. He had a hunch that streetwise kids could make it the way he had—by starting their own businesses. They were tough, assertive and used to taking risks. What if the high energy levels some of them invested in illegal, destructive behavior could be channeled into entrepreneurship?

Because he cared about kids, Mariotti left his import/export business, gave up his yuppie lifestyle and became a business teacher in a ghetto high school.

To his great frustration, he found that "business" in the public schools meant typing and bookkeeping. The kids were bored and so was Mariotti. But whenever he insisted that he had a better idea, Mariotti was told to stick to the text. "The system doesn't want real entrepreneurship," he says, "because it's so hard to control. Entrepreneurs need to get out into the world and act."

Using his own savings, Mariotti set up the nonprofit National Foundation for Teaching Entrepreneurship and he was finally hired by a principal who understood and supported his program. That led to contracts with schools throughout the city.

Mariotti's students learn real-world skills like product development, marketing techniques and financial planning. They've started dozens of new companies, ranging from chore services to rap songwriting. Mariotti sees them helping with the economic regeneration of their neighborhoods. As his program succeeds, his motives haven't changed: "It's not about making money," he says. "It's about making these kids' lives better."

As for himself, he'll tell you, "When I come home from working, I feel great. I never used to feel that good when I was just making money."

It's easy to be caring in the abstract, to just *think* compassionately. But the kind of compassion I'm talking about is *active*—it goes past good thoughts to good action. Mariotti and Lewis didn't just open their hearts—they put themselves on the line to provide practical help.

It wasn't easy for either of them. Mariotti started by seeing the world through his attackers' eyes, something most people would find hard to do. When he began his work with kids, he had to deal with a bureaucracy that blocked him again and again. Lewis dealt every day with people who could have stolen what little she had—or put her in the hospital. She also went door-to-door begging for money to keep "Grandma's House" open. Their active compassion took time, effort and courage. Sometimes the risks can be physical, but more often they're emotional—you can be rejected, and you may fail.

Moving compassion from theory to action means doing some things that, for most people, aren't easy ~

~ *Putting yourself in other people's shoes*—seeing the world through their eyes. The more different they are from you, the harder this is. Doing this won't magically close any distance you may feel from them, but it *will* help you dispel prejudices that feed distrust and conflict. ("Kids from that school are all snobs." "People who dress like that are losers." "Those people are always stupid.")

Think of people you don't want to associate with. Think of one admirable thing about each of them. Do you have *anything* in common with them? Are you willing to find out more about them? What would it be like to *be* them?

~ *Seeing people as fellow humans, not as objects to be manipulated.* Caring people understand and respect the fact that everybody has feelings and the right to be treated kindly. They don't "use" anyone to achieve their own ends. They look at others with an eye for common interests and for positive traits rather than zeroing in on differences and faults.

Have you ever taken the risk of befriending someone your friends think isn't cool? If you have, why did you? What happened?

~ *Allowing the possibility that an opponent could become an ally.* Their opposition may be rooted in a misunderstanding or a lack of information. You could be giving up a chance to defuse a conflict and make an ally.

If that change is ever to happen, you'll probably have to risk the first move. Try opening a conversation on something noncontroversial that might be a shared interest. Invite the person to join you in doing something you both like to do—playing a game, studying for a test, going to a movie. Doing something together can give you a chance to see more agreeable sides of each other. Once you're both more at ease and have established some trust, you both have a better chance of talking openly about whatever it is that divides you and seeing if you can come to some agreement.

Do you have any friends now who were once "enemies"? If you do, what caused the change? Do you have an opponent now that you could get on better terms with? Would you want to if you could? How could you go about it?

*~ Listening—without judging.*

Think of a time, perhaps when you were feeling down, when someone really listened to you, not to tell you what's wrong with you—just listening. What was the situation? What difference did that person's listening make for you? Have you ever listened that way to somebody? What was *that* situation? In both cases, what effect did this kind of listening have on the relationship?

◆••••••••••••••••••••••••••••••••••••••••••••••••••◆

*~ Following through.* Active compassion is rarely a one-time thing. It usually takes more than one caring action to help someone through a difficult time, or to build a trusting relationship. Say the new girl on the team blows an important point and the whole team is furious. You can see she feels awful about it so you say something caring to her like, "I know how you feel. You should have seen me when we lost to Jefferson and it was all my fault." That's good, but it'll be even better if you go find her the next day and ask her how she's doing. And better still if you talk your teammates into letting up on her, maybe giving her some friendly pointers on how to make the play she missed, and making sure she's included when the team goes out for pizza.

*~ Doing small favors.* I live down a long, winding dirt road with 15 other families on it; some of them have always been friendly, some not. Visitors to all our houses are constantly getting lost, so I decided to make a detailed map showing how to reach all 16 houses. I gave copies to everyone on the road so their visitors wouldn't get lost. It was fun and that was enough. But the next time I was out patching potholes, almost everyone came out to help—working with people they normally didn't talk to. There was a new friendly spirit

39

that felt good to everybody, and there's no doubt that little map helped cause it.

~ *Acknowledging people for their strengths and contributions.*

Think of a time someone acknowledged you for something you did and a time when you acknowledged someone. How did it feel to get that recognition? How did it feel to give it?

◆•••••••••••••••••••••••••••••••••••••••••••••••••••••••••◆

~ *Caring for yourself.* Give yourself credit for all the times you've done the right thing, whatever the results. Don't beat yourself up over past mistakes.

Have you ever really celebrated a personal accomplishment, or even given yourself a simple pat on the back? What did you do?

◆•••••••••••••••••••••••••••••••••••••••••••••••••••••••••◆

## Why Care? Why Act?

We can always come up with plenty of reasons for *not* putting our compassion into action, for just letting it be a good intention. We're too busy or too angry, we don't have the qualifications or the resources needed, we're too young or too old—always too something. The reasons not to act are all too easy to come up with, easier than coming up with reasons to make a caring move. But thinking about compassionate actions while sitting on our butts doesn't cut it.

Think of a time when you had an opportunity to act compassionately, but you didn't. What was the situation and why didn't you act? Think of a time when you've done something compassionate, despite the effort or risk. What did you do? Why did you do it? What were the results?

●••••••••••••••••••••••••••••••••••••••••••••••••••●

Here are the reasons *I* think it's important to care and to act on that caring ~

**1** **Active compassion makes a difference.**
There've been times when I've stepped forward to act on my compassion—and times when I've run in the other direction. But when I've made the caring move, I've seen for myself that *active compassion is one of the few things that can change a situation for the better*—even in conflicts.

*A simple act of compassion can shift the atmosphere toward cooperative solutions.*

My experience is that when people avoid important challenges, it's not because the problems themselves are that difficult; it's because people's anger, fear and frustration make it impossible for them to trust each other enough to work things out. They can't stop seeing each other as opponents, which blinds them to opportunities for solutions that might be right in front of them.

Here's where active compassion comes in: *the best way I've ever found to defuse negative emotions and end conflict is to actively care for opponents*, putting aside my negative feelings and putting myself in their shoes. A simple act of compassion can open channels of communication and shift the atmosphere away from conflict and toward cooperative solutions that simply couldn't be seen before. The people opposing you won't expect your caring, and your courage in expressing it could amaze them into responding.

Think of the story of Grandma Edie. When she said, "Kindness kills them," she was talking about defusing years of rage and pain in kids who'd received very little kindness in their lives. She could see the world through their eyes, and understand the reasons for their anger and hurt.

When helping people resolve conflicts, I've seen strikes avoided when union leaders and company officials came to understand and care about the pressures both sides were facing. I've seen bitter land-use disputes solved when environmentalists and developers were brave enough to put themselves in each others' shoes. And I remember an awful battle between my teenage son and me over doing the dishes—it ended when we were able to talk honestly about the real concerns that were beneath this silly argument and to begin to see ourselves from each other's point of view.

### Warning!

Active compassion should never be tried as a ploy to manipulate people, play on their emotions or trick them. If you *pretended* to care, you would fail—and you'd deserve to. *Active compassion works because it's real.*

Have you ever seen a conflict avoided or resolved because somebody—maybe you—had the courage to actively care for an "opponent"? What happened?

**2** **Active caring can open doors, even in big organizations.**
Let me share a secret: the key to dealing with big organizations, no matter how bureaucratic they may seem, is remembering that they're made up of individuals—people who want to be treated with caring and respect, in an environment in which they may be treated like parts in a machine. Treat them compassionately and you'll be amazed by how well they respond. As a State Department employee, I met with hundreds of people. My attitude toward them got a lot more helpful when they treated me as a person—not just as someone who might do them a favor. And I closed down very quickly to anyone who assumed that I was the enemy or some dull bureaucrat without a life.

Think of a time when you had to deal with someone in a big organization, maybe the Department of Motor Vehicles or a large store. How did it go? What was your attitude and what effect did it have on the person you dealt with?

◆ ⋯⋯⋯⋯⋯⋯⋯⋯⋯⋯⋯⋯⋯⋯⋯⋯⋯⋯⋯⋯⋯ ◆

**3** **Active compassion improves our own lives.**
Think about Scrooge in the famous Christmas story. Scrooge came to realize that without compassion our lives are isolated and unhappy. The movie *Groundhog Day* is a modern story making the same point: Bill Murray's character slowly, slooowly learns that active compassion produces meaning and happiness in his life and in the lives around him—instead of the discord and loneliness he created by being cynical and manipulative.

### "But that's not the way it works in *my* world!"

Many people agree that active compassion is a good thing, but then say that a person just can't act that way in the "real world" or they'll get run over. Then you get the descriptions of the selfish classmate, the nasty boss, the bad-tempered teacher. Everyone seems to have someone like that in mind.

There are obviously some uncaring people in Grandma Edie's world and in Steve Mariotti's. I've dealt with a few villains myself. I wasn't the kind of diplomat who works in nice clean embassies in Paris and London—my work involved wars, revolutions and arms sales, which meant dealing with some of the most uncaring people in the world. To them, I was uncaring too.

I did change. I slowly came to realize that most of these conflicts were preventable and unnecessary. I saw that humans would never end conflicts, personal or global, until we were more compassionate toward each other, and learned to put that compassion into action. I began to put myself in the shoes of the people I had to deal with, and then to risk being more compassionate toward at least some of them. As I saw my compassionate actions actually help settle conflicts, I got braver about caring. And I learned something that's now been confirmed for me a thousand times over: the risks of acting compassionately are well worth taking.

*Suspend your doubts and give compassionate action a real shot.*

It's natural to be skeptical about dealing compassionately with someone who's opposing you. But to experience how active compassion can work in your life, you've got to risk giving it a serious chance. If you're convinced such an approach will never work, any trial effort you might make will be too restrained to succeed. But if you suspend your doubts and give it a real shot, you may be amazed by the results.

It doesn't have to be a big deal—active caring can manifest in small stuff. You can start with "Hello" and a smile. Then a friendly comment about something you're likely to agree on. "Do you *believe* the homework he gave us?" Listen—really listen—to the response from this real, live fellow human being who may be as concerned as you are about doing the assignment. Realizing that you're concerned too could be the first time he's seen *you* as a fellow human with concerns he shares. Not liking the homework assignment could be the first thing you two have ever agreed on. It's a start.

It could be possible now for you to see something you honestly like about him, and to tell him so. Maybe it's just "Nice shirt." If that wasn't too hard, you might manage to do him a small favor. "I found an Internet site with some good data for that report we have to do. Here's the URL." An acknowledgement could be as simple as, "What you said in class yesterday—that really was good."

Small stuff, but as you do it, you're likely to see this person defrosting before your very eyes, becoming more likeable, and opening up to a dialogue about your differences of opinion. Experiencing this can give you the confidence to become actively compassionate as a matter of course.

You won't always receive the responses you're hoping for, but compassionate action will consistently raise the odds of resolving any conflict. And you can't really lose in trying it. Even if an "opponent" doesn't respond well, by having the courage to act with compassion in what is often an uncaring world, you're helping shape that world for the better. Someone watching you act this way—even in a "losing" effort—may be inspired to try a more compassionate approach in an entirely different situation, where somebody else will see *his* example, and on it goes.

Are there people in your life who would reject any caring action from you? How do you know this? What would happen if you tried? Are you sure?

◆ • • • • • • • • • • • • • • • • • • • • • • • • • • • • • • • • • • • • • • • • • • • • • ◆

### What's the point?
Actively caring for "opponents"
will consistently increase the chances
of finding good solutions.

**Conflict can be an addiction.** For some people, the biggest obstacle to caring isn't their opponents, it's their own need for conflict.

When the Cold War was going on between the US and the Soviet Union and I was a "Cold Warrior," I sometimes met with peace activists who wanted both sides to disarm their nuclear weapons and stop endangering the planet. Their arguments made sense, but I was amazed by how much personal hatred some of them had for the people making Cold War policy. That hatred was so intense that when people like me came to agree with them, they couldn't accept that they had won us over. They were used to dealing with enemies, but they didn't know how to react when those enemies said, "You're right. I'm with you on this." They didn't know how to win the argument and accept converts to their cause. When the Cold War ended, they were at a loss—until they found new enemies to combat.

When you act compassionately in a conflict, you begin to see that the "enemy" is the *problem* itself—not the people you're fighting. They're just fellow human beings who *could* become allies in solving the problem, provided you can build up enough trust to work with them.

Do you know people who seem to be happy only when there's something to fight about? If you do, how have you dealt with them?

◆••••••••••••••••••••••••••••••••••••••••••••••••◆

Here's the story of a Giraffe who not only accepts converts, she's devoted her life to putting her compassion for them into action ~

Peggy Schlagetter, an accomplished woman from a comfortable middle-class background, used to work as an executive secretary. Now she works with men many people would be afraid to even speak to, all of them inmates and ex-inmates of Ohio's prisons.

A survivor of a violent assault herself, Schlagetter has more reason than most to fear such men. But she says that her own assailant might be in prison somewhere and, "If he's treated like dirt...he'll end up committing another crime." Schlagetter wants to break the cycle.

She was working as a volunteer in a prison when she realized that inmates feared getting out. They worried about finding jobs, finding places to live, finding their way without constant rules and supervision. No one in the prison was helping them make the transition to useful, law-abiding lives on the "outside."

Schlagetter adapted a mentoring program she'd been using as a high school counselor and took it into maximum-security prisons. Prison officials gave her their incorrigibles, sure that she'd never crack "that joint mind set." But crack it she does. Graduates of her program, Careers in Progress (CIP), include a former thief who went on to earn his MBA and a murderer who's been law-abiding and productive for years, after prison officials swore he'd be back in a week. Schlagetter can reel off success story after success story.

CIP deals with responsibility, values, job readiness, communication skills and stress management. After inmates are released "Miss Peggy" walks them through life on the outside. She has four telephones, a hotline and a toll-free number, because she and her volunteers can be all that stands between an ex-con and the next crime. "We've talked five bank robbers out of it, so far," she says.

She says that in the beginning, "I didn't know if I wanted to take this on. I really wasn't qualified. But I think I can outdo any of these psychologists now."

Seventy-five percent of CIP grads stay out of jail, making the program a rousing success, thanks to the personal persuasive power, and the active caring, of one determined woman.

 Think of the person you find yourself in conflict with most often. Imagine a scenario in which you are actively compassionate toward that person. Imagine your caring actions melting your own negative feelings, and those of your opponent. Imagine getting to a caring, respectful solution to a longstanding conflict.

**Now *really* challenge yourself.**

**Turn that scenario into reality.**

✔ Compassion has to be more than good intentions.

✔ Moving caring from theory to action means doing some things that may be difficult ~
- ~ Putting yourself in other people's shoes, seeing the world through their eyes.
- ~ Seeing people as fellow humans, not as objects to be manipulated.
- ~ Listening.
- ~ Following through. Active compassion is rarely a one-time thing.
- ~ Allowing the possibility that an opponent could become an ally.
- ~ Doing small favors.
- ~ Acknowledging others for their strengths and contributions.
- ~ Caring for yourself.

✔ Active compassion makes a difference. It can defuse negative emotions and build the trust needed in a difficult situation.

✔ Active compassion should never be faked to manipulate people, play on their emotions or to trick them.

✔ Active compassion opens doors, even into large organizations.

✔ Active compassion improves our own lives.

✔ The risks of acting compassionately are well worth taking. To experience how it can work, give it a *serious* try.

✔ Compassionate action doesn't always bring the responses you might be hoping for, but it will raise the odds of resolving any conflict.

✔ People can become addicted to conflict. Active compassion can be an antidote to that addiction.

CHAPTER FIVE

# Risktaking and Courage: Have You Got the Nerve?

There can be risks in living a meaningful life. Whether or not you're willing to take them is one of the most important questions you'll ever face.

Ranya Kelly of Arvada, Colorado, had no idea what risks were ahead of her when she virtually fell into her life's work. She was looking for an empty carton in a dumpster behind a shoe store. Instead of empty boxes, she found hundreds of brand new shoes, thrown out by the shoe store because they hadn't sold. Kelly was delighted to salvage the shoes and take them to shelters for the homeless.

Did the shoe store thank her for finding a good use for shoes they'd thrown away as worthless? No way. They told Kelly she was a thief and threatened to have her arrested for stealing. Afraid people from the shelter might try to return the shoes to the store for cash refunds, they began putting yellow paint on the next shoes they threw out, so they couldn't be returned—or worn without embarrassment.

50

But Kelly kept pulling shoes out of the dumpster. She just cleaned off the paint, and took them to the shelters. The thought of going to jail for theft was unnerving. She not only didn't want to be locked up, she also didn't want to jeopardize her husband's position in a prominent firm. If he was fired for having a jailbird wife, it would be a disaster for her family.

In spite of all that, she kept taking the shoes. "I decided it was more important to do this work, and that if I got arrested for it, that was okay." When Kelly discovered that other shoe stores were also throwing away useable shoes, she began taking them from their dumpsters too.

Kelly stayed out of jail; she discovered that discarded goods became the property of the hauling company once they're put in a dumpster. The hauler took her side and gave her permission to take what she wanted.

Persistence paid off and that original store, plus all Denver-area stores in the same chain, now just give her the shoes without marking them with paint and without threatening her. Publicity about Kelly has inspired other stores and manufacturers to donate good stuff they would normally throw away. Kelly's crusade to prevent thoughtless waste is now moving thousands of dollars worth of goods to the poor every day of the year.

Ranya Kelly stuck her neck out to help the homeless. She wasn't a superhero or an experienced activist. Before she saw those discarded shoes, you'd say she led a pretty ordinary life. Getting thrown in jail was a serious risk for her, and so was the possibility of jeopardizing her husband's career. It took courage to face those risks.

Here's another story about seeing a problem and taking risks to do something about it ~

When David Charvat retired from a career in the Navy, he returned to Dillonvale, OH, where he'd grown up, and used his engineering know-how to run the regional sewage treatment plant. He soon discovered that the plant wasn't producing clean water—or honest reports.

Reports to the Environmental Protection Agency (EPA) said the plant had been meeting clean water standards, but Charvat learned that the plant had secretly dumped raw sewage into the Ohio River, as much as four *million* gallons a day. The sewage equipment had also been cross-connected into fresh water systems, to save money (think about *that* one!)

Charvat made changes. He authorized all employees to tell the truth to the community and he posted the EPA's phone number throughout the facility, so employees could report violations directly. In an area where some people blamed environmentalists and federal regulators for a slumping economy, Charvat became a pariah to many people, even some of his relatives. He took the heat, insisting that the plant could perform well instead of breaking the law and lying about it. Indeed, the operational changes he ordered started to improve the plant's performance.

But Charvat was threatened on the job, and rumors started at the plant and in the community impugned his integrity. A member of the plant's Board of Directors who was running for public office told Charvat to shut up or he'd be fired; Charvat told him that he'd not only keep making honest reports, but if his improvements weren't allowed to continue, he'd also blow the whistle. Charvat was fired.

That still didn't stop him. Charvat helped start activist groups to fight public health hazards and testified at hearings on sewage treatment. His efforts led to a huge fine being leveled on the sewage plant and triggered a federal program requiring states to show what actions they're taking against plants violating the Clean Water Act. And, in a happy ending to this story, Charvat was reinstated and went back to running the plant again—the right way.

If people like Kelly and Charvat were guaranteed in advance they could never get hurt, then there'd be no risk. It would be like a video game—if Ranya gets thrown in jail or David gets fired, just press the reset button and start over. But you and I know that's not the way life works. The risks that come with sticking your neck out are real.

◆••••••••••••••••••••••••••••••••••••••••••••••••••◆

### What *are* the risks?

Most of us think of physical dangers when we hear the word "risk." I've taken a lot of those. I never drove cars at 90 miles an hour, but I dodged avalanches, climbed steep mountain walls a mile high and hitchhiked around the world alone. I've had bullets whiz past my ears on three continents.

But it wasn't these physical risks that scared me—I was young, strong, quick and enjoying the adrenaline hits. The risks that really scared me—the ones I tried hardest to avoid—tested my *spirit.* They were risks like ~

~ being different—trying something new; standing up for an unpopular idea when I knew others would criticize me and I could lose friends.

~ failing, especially in public, where I could be embarrassed or ridiculed.

~ reaching out to someone who might not reach back.

~ being honest with myself about my own mistakes—and apologizing when I'd caused hurt.

These risks scared me then—and they still can. I used to think I was the only person who was afraid of such things. Other people seemed so sure of themselves. Now I know better. People may *look* confident, but they're often just as scared as you are. Risks that test the spirit are serious challenges for just about everybody.

Standing up for what you believe in means accepting the possibility—sometimes the probability—of losing friendships or your standing in your group or community. The penalties for challenging the *status quo* can be severe—the conflicts with people who like the way things are can get nasty. Public failures can be embarrassing and reactions from peers can be cruel. It takes real courage to move ahead despite such risks.

Here's a woman who moved ahead despite some hair-raising risks ~

Emma Lou Kogo watched as crack houses moved onto her street in Detroit, bringing with them a spreading cesspool of crime and addiction. "Crack devours people's lives," Kogo says. "It changes them. We saw people on our street who really cared about their children and their homes and their families all of a sudden not care about them anymore and start neglecting them... On our street we call crack 'the vampire drug'."

Kogo worked with the city's Department of Protective Services to get help for the neglected kids in the neighborhood. Again and again she stepped in to defuse abusive and volatile situations in homes torn apart by drugs. She got angry when neighborhood kids were accosted by dealers and used as drug runners. She watched in horror as a friend who had been fighting to clean up the neighborhood started using crack herself. "We just watched her go right down the drain, and we all knew that, but for the grace of God, there we were. Crack doesn't care who it gets."

At this point Kogo had to get even braver. "I'd always told my kids, 'If you don't do something about the problem, you're part of it,' so I was just practicing what I preached." She took on the dealers, determined to do whatever it took to get them off her block, as long as it was legal. She called a meeting of her neighbors.

They decided to call themselves "Just the Neighbors." They educated themselves about drugs and addiction. They contacted the police, the prosecutor's office and other agencies that could instruct or assist them. They kept each other on a positive track. "We didn't want our neighborhood destroyed by being burnt out or fighting. We wanted to be a neighborhood that cared."

Their most effective tactic was citizen surveillance. Members kept clipboards ever ready to take down the license numbers of cars pulling up to the neighborhood crack house. They made no secret of the fact that they were tracking dealers and buyers. When the Giraffe Project asked Kogo how real the danger was, she answered, "Very real. Real enough that we still don't leave our house alone. Real enough that we always know where our children are." Members of Just the Neighbors received bomb threats, had their cars tampered with and were constantly harassed. But they persevered, they stuck together, and they won back their neighborhood.

The information they gathered enabled the police and the city prosecutor to close the crack house. The occupants were evicted, and the house became the first in Detroit to be confiscated by the city under a new drug law. Just the Neighbors has gone on to help close other crack houses in the area.

Emma Lou Kogo certainly faced physical risks—*any* response to her situation would have been physically dangerous. But in choosing to respond assertively but nonviolently, she moved beyond knee-jerk fear and anger to lead her neighbors along a positive path to peace and safety in the neighborhood. It was a path that tested her spirit; Kogo stood up when others wouldn't, risked failure, reached out to people despite the dangers, and empowered an entire community to take charge of its own future.

Think of a time you've faced a risk that tested your spirit. What was the risk? What did you do? What was the result?

◆••••••••••••••••••••••••••••••••••••••••••••••••◆

### Why you?

Given the possible consequences, why should you take risks for anybody or any cause, especially if there are a lot of other people who could take it on? It's obviously easier to keep your head down, to avoid standing out from the crowd and to just hope that somebody else will fix what's wrong. OK, here are three very good reasons ~

1 Solving tough public problems takes more than wishing they were solved—it takes action. Just complaining won't change any of the things that may concern you. Change happens only when people—not superheroes, but ordinary people—see problems and do something about them, despite the risks.

When we ask Giraffes like Kelly, Charvat and Kogo why they take the risks they do, they often say they had no choice. The challenge was right in front of them, nobody else was stepping up—what else were they supposed to do? Giraffes act to make a difference in their communities and the world. The stories of Giraffes remind us that if we don't act, the problems won't get solved. The message of Giraffes' lives is, "It's up to *all* of us."

2 You can inspire others. That's why the Giraffe Project tells Giraffes' stories—so that more people will be exposed to examples of good actions, and then take such actions themselves. Sticking your neck out for the common good makes you one of those examples that cause more good to be done in the world. And that's a pretty good thing.

There aren't enough such role models. Too many people are willing to just accept whatever's going on around them, even if they don't agree with it, even if they're whining and complaining about it. Some of them have been taught to play it safe since childhood and they've never questioned that. Some just get used to a comfortable, predictable lifestyle and aren't willing to risk any of that comfort and certainty. Our media-filled culture trains people to be passive observers, watching actors deal with problems, and looking for ways to amuse ourselves rather than tackling the real-world challenges that surround us. And our media further undermine incentives to act for the common good by using the word "hero" to describe celebrities instead of people like Kelly, Charvat and Kogo who see a need and take risks to make a difference.

*Too many people are willing to just accept whatever's going on.*

At the Giraffe Project, we say that *heroes* take on serious challenges at real personal risk, to serve the common good. *Celebrities* are famous, but they're not usually heroes; they might inspire you to work on your jump shot or your guitar licks, but that's not the inspiration of a hero. *Giraffes* are heroes, inspiring us to take on difficult challenges in our communities and in the world; few of them are celebrities.

Using those Giraffe Project definitions, who are your heroes? Who are your favorite celebrities? What influence do these people have on your life?

◆••••••••••••••••••••••••••••••••••••••••••••••••••••◆

Everyone has the potential to be a positive model for others—and even modest actions count. You don't have to wait for a chance to be a big hero, taking on a huge risky challenge. Just look at the everyday events of your life and the opportunities you have to take small, positive risks that could extend your perceived limits, that could take you to a personal best in serving the common good. Step up to those opportunities and take your best shot. Your actions may inspire other people when *they're* the ones being challenged.

3 You may not be able to lead a meaningful life *without* taking risks. Committing to your ideals, being fully alive—can put you into situations that scare you. But if being fully alive is important to you, you'll take those risks. Avoiding them time after time will deaden your spirit, and can lead you into a wasteland where nothing is meaningful, where life is marking time. *Remember the zombie!*

---

## What's the point?

Leading a meaningful life
is worth the risks it may entail.

---

## How to Take Risks

There are smart ways to take risks and not-so-smart ways. Smart is better. Here are three smart suggestions ~

~ Get the facts. Find out as much as you can about the risks you face.

~ Reduce those risks by increasing your competence.

~ Focus on the *meaning* your actions have for you, so you can find the courage to face the risks that remain.

**Get the facts.**
By gathering information, you may find out that some perceived risks aren't risks at all, or are less significant than you first thought. People were afraid of eclipses when they thought they were caused

by an angry god. The risks disappeared when people learned that eclipses were predictable effects of the orbits of the moon, sun and earth. You can improve your knowledge of the risks you see by questioning people more familiar with the situation than you are, and by doing research in books, newspapers, and magazines, or on the Internet.

Have you ever been in a situation in which the risks you first perceived disappeared in the light of new information? As an example, you might be summoned to a meeting with the principal or your boss, and think that you're in trouble. Then you find out the person just wants to thank you for some job well done. If something like this has happened to you, what was it?

◆·················································◆

On the other hand if you increase your knowledge and find the risks are *real,* the things you've learned can help you prepare to take those risks.

**Increase your competence.**
Situations tend to be scarier the less competent we feel to handle them—often because we lack skills, tools, or experience. A trek through the wilderness is a lot scarier without a map. Giving a speech is more frightening if you have no idea how to do it.

Assuming there's time, you can increase your competence to face a risky situation. For example, you can ~

~ Learn and practice a skill you need, like giving a speech or a media interview.

~ Get the right tools. A computer with Web access? A pickup truck? A hand-held microphone?

~ Get advice and support from others. *Somebody* knows how to do this and can help you learn how too.

Have you ever been able to reduce a risk by increasing your competence to take it? Studying for an exam in your most difficult class is an obvious example. What else?

---

**Find your courage.**
Even with increased knowledge and competence, it's unlikely you'll be able to eliminate risks completely. Something will still remain that scares you. To face it will take courage.

Courage is not about having no fear. Only a fool is fearless.

*Courage is acting in the face of fear.*

Think of a time when you've been courageous. What did you do? What happened? Where did you find the courage?

---

**This is what I know about finding courage ~**

When something you're doing is meaningful, you feel deeply that you're on the right path, and you're committed to walking it. If you have to do something that scares you, in order to keep on that path, don't look at those risks by themselves. See them as integrated parts of this whole action you feel is meaningful. When you look at risks this way they don't go away, but they *do* seem more worth taking. The commitment you have for what you're doing spills over onto the risks you face, and you're better able to act in the face of fear—you have more courage.

Let's say you've agreed to be a literacy mentor to a young kid who's way below his grade level in reading. But you quickly see that reading is the least of it. He's angry and he's starved for affection and respect, at school and at home. You see you're not just helping with his homework. You're up on a high wire, looking at far more responsibility than you want. You don't know how to handle him when he acts out. You could foul up and make things worse.

Increasing your knowledge of the situation makes it clear that the risks are even bigger than you thought. His home life is a mess and he's flunking *everything*. So you increase your competence to deal with the problems—talking to counselors and other mentors, reading articles on listening skills, and planning activities that will help you create a bond with him. The risks remain, but you find the courage to deal with them by reflecting on what it *means* to you to be a mentor, helping shape a child's life for the better. Now you can see the risks in the context of doing something that's meaningful to you, so your inner talk can be, "Being a mentor to someone who needs one so badly is really important to me. The risks that are scaring me now are a part of the job—so here I go." You know the risks are worth taking, and you have the courage to take them.

---

### What's the point?

We can find the courage we need
by focusing on the *meaning* an action has for us.

---

Something that happened during one of my bizarre adventures illustrates the impact of meaning on courage. I was on a ship in the Gulf of Alaska that caught fire in the middle of the night. As the fire spread, 550 passengers and crew were directed into lifeboats. The lifeboat procedures were chaotic; 95 people were wedged into our boat though a big sign on the bow said it was built for 48. We were 140 miles from the Alaskan coast. People were freezing cold, and a storm was building as we waited for dawn, the earliest that rescue helicopters could arrive. There were a dozen members of the crew in that boat, including a couple of junior officers. None of them took charge. One of the seamen stood up in that jam-packed, pitching boat—a very bad idea—and screamed that we were all going to die. Several people started to weep.

*Courage*

*was*

*in order,*

*not panic.*

An elegant woman in her seventies immediately stood up next to the ranting crewman and slapped him across the face. The man shut up and stared at her, stunned, while she lectured him on his bad behavior. He sat down, red-faced. The weeping stopped. Somebody started leading songs. The moment of panic passed.

This magnificent woman was certainly aware of the extreme danger we were in. I don't think she was necessarily any less scared than the rest of us in that lifeboat, shivering and wet, watching the storm coming on. I think what separated her from the panicky crewmen was the meaning each put into that desperate situation. Even with their training and their professional responsibilities, the safety of the group, and their professional pride, seemed to mean nothing to them. When they needed to be courageous, they weren't.

But that woman was from a family with a long history of championing the common good—public service had meaning for her. Lives were at stake, so she stopped the panic, not only with her action, but also with her example. When that crewman lost it, some of the passengers started to follow his lead. But the woman led in the opposite direction, showing people that courage was in order, not panic. She reversed the mood and behavior of the group.

Do you think you're more courageous in some situations than in others? Does whether or not the situation is meaningful to you make a difference?

✔ There can be risks in living a meaningful life. Whether or not you're willing to take them is one of the most important questions you'll ever face.

✔ The risks that come with trying to solve significant problems are real.

✔ The risks that test your spirit could be harder to face than those that endanger your physical safety.

✔ Three good reasons to take risks to help solve the problems you see ~

1. Change happens only when people—not superheroes, but ordinary people—see problems and do something about them, despite the risks.

2. Your example is important. Everyone has the potential to be a positive model for others—and even modest actions count. One reason there aren't enough such models is that media confuse celebrities with genuine heroes, like Giraffes.

3. You may not be able to lead a meaningful life *without* taking risks. But if being fully alive is important to you, you'll take those risks. Avoiding them time after time will deaden your spirit, and can lead you into a wasteland where nothing is meaningful, where life is just marking time.

✔ Three good suggestions for taking risks ~

~ Get the facts. Find out as much as you can about the risks you face.

~ Reduce those risks by increasing your competence.

~ To find the courage to face the risks that remain, focus on the meaning these actions have for you.

**Not too surprisingly, the Giraffe Project
has a lot of quotes about courage.
Here are just a few—in case you need further convincing
that sticking your neck out for others is the right thing to do ~**

*Avoiding danger is no safer in the long run than outright exposure. The fearful are caught as often as the bold.* —Helen Keller

*Whatever you do you need courage. Whatever course you decide upon there is always someone to tell you you are wrong. There are always difficulties arising which tempt you to believe that your critics are right. To map out a course of action and follow it to the end requires courage... peace has its victories, but it takes brave people to win them.* —Ralph Waldo Emerson

*You gain strength, courage and confidence by every experience in which you really stop to look fear in the face... You must do the thing you think you cannot do.* —Eleanor Roosevelt

*A single, seemingly powerless person who dares to cry out the word of truth and to stand behind it with all his person and all his life, ready to pay a high price has, surprisingly, a greater power than thousands of anonymous voters.* —Vaclav Havel

*We make progress in our society only if we stop cursing and complaining about its shortcomings and we have the courage to do something about them.* —Elizabeth Kubler-Ross

*To defend oneself against a fear is simply to insure that one will, one day, be conquered by it; fears must be faced.* —James Baldwin

*Adventure without risk is Disneyland.* —Douglas Coupland

# CHAPTER SIX

# Planning Your Moves

You've chosen your issue, created a project to address the issue, formed a vision of the results you want, and found the compassion and courage you'll need to move forward. Now it's time to make a plan and put it into action.

**Plans are boring?** If imagination, spontaneity, vision and enthusiasm were all you needed to carry out a service project, there'd be a lot more successful projects. If you *really* want to get a project done right, especially one that involves a lot of people and details, you need to back up these qualities with some solid planning. Sure, planning may not be the most exciting thing to do in the world, and it takes time, patience and intense thinking, but… *A good plan will keep you organized and focused, help you make the most of your time and energy, and increase your chances of getting good results.*

Have you ever worked on an activity or project in which nobody seemed to be handling the details, or anticipating next steps? What happened? How did you feel?

The planning method you'll see here has been tested for years in many different situations, and it works. It's written to apply to a group project, but you can easily adapt it for working on your own.

Here are the steps:

    **1** REVIEW THE ISSUE, THE PROJECT AND THE VISION.

    **2** GET MORE INFORMATION.

    **3** RECRUIT ANY HELP YOU NEED.

    **4** CREATE AN ACTION PLAN.

    **5** PUT YOUR PLAN—AND YOURSELF—IN GEAR.

    **6** ASSESS PROGRESS AS YOU GO.

**1** **REVIEW THE ISSUE, THE PROJECT AND THE VISION.** Get out the two posters you've made (pages 21 and 30). Confirm that your group still agrees on the issue, the project, the vision and the details—and that they're committed to going forward with the project.

**2** **GET MORE INFORMATION**
**Identify the key people who can have an effect on your project.** Review your initial information on people whose lives will be affected by this project—the "stakeholders," (page 18). Any others to add now? If you've identified people already working on this problem, talk to them. Would it make sense to join them or to coordinate your efforts? Who are the people whose *decisions* could affect your project—people whose support or opposition would make a difference?

> In the Lake McChubb example, these might include the Mayor, the head of the Health Department, the head of the Department of Parks, and the Chair of the Lake McChubb Homeowners' Association.

Don't forget the media—they can do a lot to influence people. Your list of key people should include local editors and reporters who might cover a project like yours. Use the tips in Chapter Eight for developing a media strategy.

Ask the people you contact for their advice on anyone else you should be talking to.

If you think that any of these key people are potential opponents, don't write them off. Instead, think of ways to get them involved in a part of the project that might interest them. Getting them on board early is a lot easier than trying to enlist their support or approval later on, when their opposition may have hardened. See Chapter Nine for tips on finding common ground.

**Identify obstacles and risks.** Obstacles are problems that require thinking, work, and sometimes money, to overcome. Risks are things that scare you. Some things, such as giving a speech, might be both an obstacle and a risk. Write down every obstacle and risk for your project that you can think of. If you looked at potential obstacles when you created a vision for your project (pages 29-30), include them here. The list for the Lake McChubb group might include:

&ast; We'll have to do things we've never done before, and we could make fools of ourselves.

&ast; We still don't have enough information.

&ast; Someone might object to what we want to do, and try to stop us.

&ast; We need more money, tools and supplies than we thought.

&ast; Not everybody in our group is exactly enthusiastic about this.

&ast; We need more time than we have.

**Identify resources.** Now write down all the *resources* you can think of, including those you've already got or can get. Here's McChubb's list:

&ast; Us—we're smart, competent and enthusiastic.

&ast; Donations from local businesses and service clubs, such as Rotary.

&ast; Things we can bring from home.

&ast; The library and the Internet.

&ast; Training or coaching from local experts.

**Get any additional information you need.** It could be some technical data, or some advice on fundraising. Use the library and the Internet. Ask people who have the skills, knowledge and experience you need.

**Brainstorm possible solutions.** Look at the obstacles and risks and see how many of them you can cover with the resources you've identified. For example, if one obstacle is: "We need more money, tools and supplies than we thought," a solution might include "Donations from local businesses and service clubs such as Rotary." If you're worried about failing on things you've never done before, then get some training or coaching in whatever those things are. Continue brainstorming possible solutions—don't limit yourself just to the resources you've already identified. Think of the solutions to obstacles you came up with when you created a vision for your project (page 30). Some or all of them should help you now.

Come up with a couple of possible solutions for each obstacle or risk you see. Write them down.

**3** RECRUIT ANY HELP YOU NEED. If at this point you see that your project is too big for you or your group, or if you need specialized help—for example, someone with graphic arts skills—then you may need to recruit other people.

Start by asking people you already know. If that's not enough, ask to speak at meetings of organizations that might be interested in your issue. Put a call for help in their newsletters. Organize your own recruiting meeting if you have to.

You'll attract allies by the strength of your commitment and ideas. But it's your vision that will have the most power to get people excited about how they can help. So before you try to recruit more people, see again in your mind the picture of the results you want.

**4** CREATE AN ACTION PLAN. An action plan will keep you on course and on schedule as you work on your project. It's open to change and refinement, but check each suggested entry or change against the vision for your project. If a new idea doesn't help fulfill the vision, it doesn't belong in the plan.

Make a third poster headlined, "Action Plan." Draw a horizontal "timeline" across the top. The left end of the line represents the day your project starts and the right end marks the day it is to end.

Break your project down into no more than six or seven goals, each one the accomplishment of a part of the project. When all the goals are reached, the project will be complete.

A good way to come up with goals is to look at ~

~ The details you've already described for your project.

~ The obstacles and risks you've already identified.

~ The possible solutions you've brainstormed.

If you know that the project will require money to cover expenses, then one goal will be raising that money. If getting the word out will be important to the success of your project, then a goal should be to create and carry out a media strategy (see Chapter 8).

Make sure that the goals, taken together, get all the jobs done that need to get done, but don't repeat each other. List the goals down the left side of the action plan poster, leaving space between them. See the "Scrub McChubb" action plan that follows page 70.

Most goals will be complex enough so that you'll want to break them down further, into steps. For example, under a goal for raising money, steps might be ~

~ Create a budget. (See page 70.)

~ Find out who gives money.

~ Send letters to potential funders and/or visit them.

~ Organize and carry out three car washes.

Write the steps underneath each goal. Now draw a horizontal time-line next to each step. Put the right end of the timeline on the day when you know that step has to be finished if the whole project is to be done on time. Estimate how long that step will take to carry out. Using that information, count backwards to the day work on that step must start—that's the left end of the timeline.

When you've finished, coordinate the timelines to make sure that any actions that must be completed before others can start are done on time. For example, fundraising steps will have to be completed before you can buy supplies.

Finally, you might want to add marks on each timeline to note important events—for example, for the step "organize and carry out three car washes," you might want to use these "benchmarks" to mark the three Saturdays when you'll hold car washes.

On the next page there's a simplified version of an action plan for the "Scrub McChubb" project. The real thing would have all the steps written in and all the benchmarks (most now just marked with a ✔) described. It would also be a lot messier.

**Sign people up for jobs.** If you're in a group, the final part of creating your action plan is to work out who takes responsibility for completing each of its steps. With a little patience, your group can match most steps with people interested in working on them. If there's a specific job or two that nobody wants to do, however, then draw straws or have people take turns.

All the people working on the same step are a team. Some might be members of more than one team. Some steps might be small enough for one person to do. Your group can figure all this out. When you've got it, write down who's doing what on the action plan poster.

Pat yourself on the back when your action plan is finished. It's not an easy task but it's important and you did it. Before the work actually starts, review the plan one more time.

**Create a budget.** If your project requires money then the fundraising goal in your action plan must be based on a budget. Budgets are estimated expenses matched against estimated sources of cash income. The cash income must equal or exceed the expenses. A budget should also list items given to you ("in-kind contributions"). See the example on the back of the next page.

# Scrubb McChubb Action Plan

| Timeline | Jan | Feb. | March | April | June |
|---|---|---|---|---|---|

**Goal 1** To work with local residents, getting their advice and support.

*meetings scheduled* ✔   *1st meeting* ✔   *2nd meeting* ✔

Step1
Organize and implement a series of public meetings.
(Ann, Tyler, Kendra)

*campaign organized* ✔   *campaign launched* ✔

Step2
Organize and implement a campaign to visit every house in the neighborhood. (Miranda, Karen)

**Goal 2** To coordinate with city officials, local environmentalists and others.
Step1    ✔
Step2    ✔    ✔

**Goal 3** To pick up trash, replace trash cans, and remove graffiti from benches and trees along the shore.
Step1    ✔

**Goal 4** To create and carry out a media strategy to help spread the word on what citizens can do.
Step1    ✔    ✔
Step2    ✔    ✔    ✔

**Goal 5** To talk to local nurseries and hardware stores about putting more warnings on house and garden products that add pollution to the lake and about suggesting alternative, less-polluting products.
Step1    ✔    ✔    ✔
Step2    ✔

**Goal 6** To raise money needed for printing and supplies.
Step1    ✔    ✔    ✔
Step2    ✔
Step3    ✔
Step4    ✔

# Budget for "Scrub McChubb"

| Item | Estimated expenses |
|---|---|
| printing flyers | $350 |
| travel (gas) | $50 |
| trash bags | $75 |
| postage | $75 |
| other supplies and miscellaneous | $50 |
| **Total Expenses** | **$600** |

| Item | Estimated cash income |
|---|---|
| Rotary Club donation | $300 |
| other donations | $150 |
| car wash receipts | $200 |
| **Total Cash income** | **$650** |

| Item | Estimated In-kind Contributions |
|---|---|
| free ads in newspaper | $400 |
| trash cans (from hardware store) | $150 |
| **Total In-kind Contributions** | **$550** |

**5** PUT YOUR PLAN—AND YOURSELF—IN GEAR. No plan is worth much if it just stays on the shelf. Your plan is an *action* plan—so now's the time to bring it off the drawing board and into the real world.

**6** ASSESS PROGRESS AS YOU GO. As the work proceeds, it's important that you regularly assess progress, discuss solutions to problems that come up and make any necessary course corrections. If you're working in a group, the best way to assess is in regular group meetings. The sessions might start with questions like these ~

~ Is the work on each step going forward on schedule?

~ Is everyone completing the work he or she signed up to do?

~ Do any of the work assignments need to be adjusted?

~ Do any *new* steps need to be added to the plan?

Go beyond the nuts-and-bolts. Ask yourselves ~

~ Is the project easier or harder than we thought it would be? Why?

~ Have there been unexpected events or lessons? What were they? What's your reaction to them? What are the implications for what we do next?

~ What does this project mean to us now, and has that changed? If so, why?

If at any point your effort seems to be losing momentum, stopping, going backwards, or heading off in too many directions—bring it back on course by reviewing your vision. Thinking about and talking about the vision will rekindle its power to guide, inspire and keep your group together.

Assessment meetings are also a good time to bring in outside resources for any additional training or guidance that might be needed. For example, you could invite a reporter from a local paper or television station to coach you on how to get media attention.

## FUNDRAISING!

Most projects require some money. If your budget is small, say under $300, then tried-and-true methods like car washes, rummage sales, spaghetti dinners, pancake breakfasts, bake sales, walk-a-thons and bike-a-thons should work just fine. But if the sums you need are larger than that, then you may want to apply for contributions from companies, foundations, or service clubs such as Rotary and Kiwanis. This section is about *that* kind of fundraising.

*How much money will you need?*

**Find out who gives money.** Start by finding out which local service clubs or companies give grants for projects like yours. Ask people who are members or employees, or who belong to other groups that have received such grants.

Foundations also give grants. You can find out about them on the Internet or by using directories you'll find in the library. You need to know which ones give money for projects like yours and where to send for their brochures and application forms. Getting a grant from a foundation takes more time than from a local service club or company. Small local foundations may respond to your request within a month or two. Apply to larger ones only if your project requires a lot of money and will continue for a year or more. Big national foundations give larger grants, but it can take six to nine months to get a decision from them, and your proposal would be one of thousands they receive.

Whether it's service clubs, companies or foundations you're looking at, get the detailed information and applications you need. If the description of their interests matches up with what you want to do, apply. Follow all instructions; if they say your application can be four pages max, don't send six. It's perfectly OK to apply to more than one potential donor at once for the same project—just tell all of them where else you've applied.

**Make a personal contact.** The chances of getting a contribution go way up if you can talk to someone at the organization about your request. The easiest way to do this is to find someone who has a contact there and can introduce you.

If you don't have that kind of personal connection, pick up the phone. Ask for an appointment with the person who makes funding decisions, if the organization is local. If it's far away, ask to speak to that person on the phone. "Cold calls" like these may be scary, but you may well find the person on the other end of the line friendlier than you expected. Well-thought-out, grass-roots service projects are attractive to funders and people may be delighted to talk to a concerned, active young person—especially if they're used to thinking people your age don't care.

*Talk to someone personally about your request.*

When you write a funding request ~

- ~ Start your proposal with a short summary, unless you're using a foundation form that doesn't require it.
- ~ Describe the problem you want to solve, simply, clearly and without exaggerating.
- ~ Present your clear, sharp vision of how things will look when your project is completed.
- ~ Describe your plan for reaching that vision.
- ~ Say why your group is competent to implement the plan.
- ~ Include a simple budget and ask for an amount of money that your research says is a normal amount for that donor.
- ~ Tell them how you'll know whether your project worked or not.

**Follow up.** When you get a grant, send an immediate thank-you letter. As you use the money, observe all requirements set forth in the grant. Send progress reports even if they're not required.

If you get a turndown letter that shows that someone at least thought about your request, send back a note thanking the organization for considering it. You'll be adding to the courtesy in the world—and the people who get it will remember that note if you apply again.

✔A good plan will keep you organized and focused, help you make the most of your time and energy, and increase your chances of getting good results.

✔ The basic steps are ~

**1.** Review the issue, the project and the vision of what you want to accomplish.

**2.** Identify the key people who can influence your project, the obstacles and risks you might face, the resources you've got or can get, and any other factors that could affect your success. Brainstorm possible solutions to the obstacles and risks.

**3.** Recruit any help you need.

**4.** Create an action plan. Break your project down into no more than six or seven goals. Each goal represents a piece of the action, accomplishing one part of the project. Most goals can themselves be broken down into more detailed steps. Draw a "timeline" for each step showing when work on it starts and when it ends. Create a budget, if your project requires money. Finally, work out who will do all the jobs represented by the steps in your action plan.

**5.** Go for it! Put your plan—and yourself—into gear.

**6.** Assess progress as you go.

✔ If your project's budget requires fundraising, you can apply for contributions from companies, foundations, or service clubs such as Rotary and Kiwanis. Research potential sources of funds. Try to develop personal contacts at funding sources. In your written application, describe the problem you want to solve, your group's competence for solving it, and your vision.

CHAPTER SEVEN

# It's Up to You:
# Taking Responsibility
# and Making Decisions

Does it seem like every adult in your life is telling you to be "responsible"? The adults in my life certainly were. What they meant was staying out of trouble and meeting their expectations, like doing homework and chores on time. It was not something I wanted to hear a lot about.

I have a different view of responsibility now. I see it as a lot more than avoiding foul-ups and meeting other people's expectations—it's a powerful way to create positive change. But to get that powerful effect, you have to expand the concept of being responsible to cover not just your behavior, but your *attitudes* as well.

Attitudes may influence people and events as much as behavior does. Think about times when you, or someone else in your family, comes home after a very bad day or a very good one. The evening for the entire family can be affected by that one person's attitude. Notice the power of a teacher to set the mood for an entire class. And we've all been in groups in which one angry person, annoyed by some trivial thing like a broken pencil or a lost direction, manages to spoil everybody's day. The fact is, *every* situation is affected by both the behavior and attitudes of the people involved, whether it's in a class, a family, a club, a meeting, a sports team, or any other group you can think of.

Have you ever been in a situation in which the attitude or behavior of just one person has changed the mood of an entire group, positively or negatively? If so, what happened? Have *you* ever been that one person? If so, how did that happen; what did you do?

◆••••••••••••••••••••••••••••••••••••••••••••••••••◆

Look at any situation you're in as if it were a stage play, with you as one of the actors. Every one of your actions and attitudes helps write the script for that play, whether you see it or not and whether you like it or not. If what you contribute to the script is anger, blame, cynicism, fear, or hopelessness, then you push the final act of the play in that direction. On the other hand, if the behavior and attitudes you bring to that situation are caring, courageous and hopeful, you'll influence events in that direction.

---

### What's the point?

Given that our behavior and attitudes always affect the people and events around us, it just makes sense for us to be more conscious of both—to understand that we're on the stage and not in the audience.

---

Consider being in a club or a class in which you have to deal with people who think differently than you do, and who perhaps make you uncomfortable. It's in your interest to check your attitudes before going into such a situation, so you can take responsibility for them as well as for your behavior—and change both if that's what you need to do. Are you dragging in any emotional baggage, any prejudices or old grudges? Are you upset or angry from something totally unrelated to that meeting, such as a fight with a friend that morning? If you *don't* take responsibility for those negative attitudes—by curbing them and the behavior they might prompt—they're almost sure to show through in your body language, and to undercut your persuasiveness, patience or good judgment.

*Your being responsible could improve what happens.*

It's just as important to take responsibility for *positive* behavior and attitudes. At that difficult club meeting, for example, taking responsibility could mean cooling a conflict with your good humor, bringing up a difficult subject with respect and sensitivity, or offering a caring word or gesture to someone who's hurting. In ways like these you'll inspire others to their best behavior through *your* best behavior. Your being responsible could decisively improve what happens.

### Be conscious of the little things.
Part of accepting this broader kind of responsibility is sweating the small stuff. How you answer the phone, meet people, wait in line, introduce newcomers or even answer a roll call, can affect the mood of everyone who sees or hears you. If in these little things you're distracted, unfriendly, sarcastic or critical, it can push other people's moods in that direction. If, on the other hand, you handle these little things with caring, respect and humor, you're helping create a positive atmosphere.

Think of some routine interaction you have with another person. Maybe it's the woman who serves the French fries in the school cafeteria—always frowning—or your little brother, who never does his share of the dishes. Consciously make your response to that person warmer and more positive than usual. Maybe nothing happens the first few times you do this, but look again after you've kept it up awhile. See any changes?

**Take responsibility for the effects of your communications.**

You have an effect on each person you deal with, and you have to be thinking about that, especially if the people you're talking to are different from you—and no two people are the same. Laughing and yelling, "Hey dude, move your butt!" may be a good way to try to speed up a friend, but it wouldn't work too well with a teacher or a boss. A note written on the back of an old homework sheet is fine if you're reminding a friend to return the hat you loaned him last week. But it would be the wrong way to ask the head of the Kiwanis Club for a donation. Email can be *very* informal—so you've got to be especially mindful of who your readers might be before you press "Send." Finally, watch spelling, grammar and neatness in written communications. Sloppy, misspelled, ungrammatical writing can definitely sabotage your chances of getting the result you want.

*It may be unwise to yell "Hey dude, move your butt!" at a teacher.*

These examples are pretty obvious. But now let's fine-tune. Does anyone you're talking to have sensitivities you should be concerned about—maybe political or religious beliefs that might require more than the usual care in choosing your language? Are you talking to someone who's learning English and might not get your jokes? To someone who often needs directions repeated?

The better you get to know people as individuals and the more you can put yourself in their shoes, the better you'll communicate with them. But this is about more than communicating—it's about taking responsibility for your impact on others, and it's a measure of your respect for them.

**Don't send mixed messages.**

Watch for inconsistencies between the content of your words and your tone of voice and body language. Have you ever heard people make "happy" statements about something when their faces were sad and their voices so quiet you could barely hear them? What about a guy who tells you he's not mad but his face is the color of a tomato and he looks like he's ready to put his fist through the wall? Then there's the person who says she's all for your idea, but you have a hard time believing her when her narrowed eyes and her hostile tone of voice say "shark" instead of "friend."

Try this exercise: Look in the mirror and think of a message that expresses a strong like or dislike, then deliver it with exaggerated body language that says the opposite of your words. You could tell the mirror you love the band whose music you hate the most, and see how many ways you can put "yuk" in your voice, face and movements. Exaggerating this way can help you avoid sending mixed messages in a real situation, and make you more aware of such messages when you receive them.

Have you ever talked to someone whose words said one thing while their gestures, expressions or tone of voice "said" something completely different? What was the effect on you? Have *you* ever said one thing while your nonverbal communication said another? What was the result?

**You may not see every result of your being responsible.**
You can influence someone else by your words or example and never hear about it. It could be some shy kid who sees you speak up in a difficult moment. Weeks later, she remembers and does the same thing, and you'll never know it was because she saw what you did.

Have you ever been inspired by someone else's words or behavior—and never told them that? What was the situation?

## What's the point?
Every move you make—or don't make—
and every attitude you bring into a situation
could and probably *will* influence the outcome.
This happens both positively and negatively,
and whether you see it or not.

That's a tough thing to accept, because it means that you're constantly "on duty," that even something you might think is a minor act or a momentary attitude can have effects that go beyond your own life. But being that responsible is a powerful way to positively shape the results of any situation you're in. You don't have to be megasmart or highly experienced to do this. Most people aren't aware of the power of taking responsibility in this deeper way. All you have to do is take responsibility for both your actions and your attitudes—and watch how that changes your world.

**Taking responsibility *matters.***
There are challenges at every level of our lives—personal, home, school, community, national, world—many of them seem huge and unmanageable. It's natural to ask, "What difference can I make?"

When we realize that every action and every attitude *can* make a difference, and we're acting on that realization, we can consciously change relationships, organizations, communities—and beyond. History is full of people who were responsible in this way, and who made a difference despite the odds. The Giraffe Project honors only living people, so this man hasn't been commended as a Giraffe, but there's no doubt he was a genuine hero, one who took responsibility on an amazing scale ~

Raoul Wallenberg was a Swedish diplomat sent into Budapest by the US War Refugee Board in the summer of 1944 to rescue Jews from the Gestapo. It was late in the war, millions of Jews had already been killed, and the extermination operation seemed unstoppable. Many a would-be rescuer had gone to the gas chambers with them.

Wallenberg was a new player in the deadly game and he didn't play by the Nazis' rules; he had his own and they were light years away from anything an SS thug could understand. How could they cope with an adversary whose role models were Charlie Chaplin and the Marx Brothers? Wallenberg mixed absurdity with audacity, giving him a bizarre power to bluff, bribe and out-maneuver the Nazis.

Wallenberg knew that his adversaries had an inordinate respect for authority and official documents—and zero sense of humor. Early on, he got permission to issue Swedish protective passports to 1,500 people. While he was asking formally for permission to issue a thousand more, he was actually printing thousands more. These wholly bogus documents were loaded down with so many "official" seals and crests that normal people would immediately think they were fake. Not the SS. They thought they were real. So Wallenberg printed up more. And more.

Within weeks, 400 Jews were staffing Wallenberg's operation, none of them wearing the required Star of David. Wallenberg set up safe houses all over the city festooned with Swedish flags and guarded by young, blond Jewish men wearing Nazi uniforms. In the streets of Budapest, there were "Swedes" everywhere, many of them wearing the hats, beards and earlocks of the Orthodox.

Survivors of those terrifying times tell astonishing stories about Wallenberg bursting into a courtyard where Jewish families were huddled in one corner, Nazi machine gunners taking aim at them from the other. Radiating authority and shouting commands in German, Wallenberg planted himself in front of the families and ordered the gunners to leave. And they did. Wallenberg raced to a death train loaded with Jews, climbing the side of a boxcar and running along the roofs, opening the air vents and dropping in his bogus Swedish identity papers. He then ordered the troops in charge to release all Swedes. And they did. Heroism à la Groucho and Charlie.

Wallenberg is credited with saving more than 100,000 men, women and children. But he did not save himself. When Soviet troops were approaching the city, Wallenberg went to meet with their commanding officer, and never returned.

---

## What's the point?

Putting ideals into action and leading a meaningful life
are not easy.
There are tough problems and people out there
and they're not going to change overnight.
Acknowledge these realities
but know that there is great power
in taking responsibility
for your attitudes as well as your actions.

---

## Making Decisions

An important part of being responsible is facing up to decisions when you have to make them, and then making the best ones you can. It's easy to make bad decisions, especially when you're under time pressures, experiencing conflicting priorities or feeling strong emotions. Here's a story about doing it wrong ~

In the summer of my junior year in college, seven members of the college mountaineering club climbed Mt. McKinley's north wall, a first ascent straight up the center of one of the most dangerous mountain faces in the world. We'd come down the mountain and circled around to our original base camp. From there, it was a long hike across the Alaskan wilderness to our van. It had taken us three days to pack in the month before; now, our heads filled with thoughts of steaks and hot showers, we crossed the mosquito-infested wilderness in just two. When we reached the McKinley River in late afternoon, we could see our van on the far bank, less than a half-mile away.

The water level in glacier-fed rivers like the McKinley varies dramatically, depending on the time of day. Sunlight had hit the mountain's glaciers in the early afternoon. Now the meltwater was at its height, roaring past us—the river was in full flood. There's a prime directive in crossing rivers near glacier-covered mountains— "Wait until low water," which usually means early morning. When the sun disappears, the snow and ice on mountains stops melting into the rivers and they become shallower and slower-moving.

*We thought*

The smart decision would have been to catch some sleep on the riverbank, then cross at first light. But we remembered that the manager of the McKinley Park Hotel had made a public bet that we would never climb the north wall and live to tell about it. If our "damfool" idea succeeded, we could have all the steak dinners we could eat—on the house. His hotel was less than an hour away, and after six weeks of rice and beans, we could smell those steaks.

*we were*

*indestructible.*

We looked at the river, almost waist-high and roaring so loudly we had to scream in each other's ears to be heard. What to do? We'd just done something no other climbers had ever done. We thought we were indestructible. And we wanted our steaks.

We roped up and started across the eleven braided streams that formed the river. The weight of our packs helped us keep our footing as we crossed the first ten streams.

Hank Abrons and I were the last pair to reach the final braid. Hank plunged in and was almost across when I started in. Almost at once I stepped in a hole that the others had somehow missed, lost my balance and was dragged under. I struggled to get my face above water, gasping for air, but my pack had now become a deadly anchor. Tons of fast-moving water pummeled me against rocks on the stream bottom. Swimming was impossible. Hank had made it to the far bank but was pulled off his feet by the rope that joined us, and was being dragged backward across the gravel toward the flood. The others were too far away to help in time. In the next 30 seconds, either the pull of the rope would pendulum me onto the far bank—or the force of the river propelling me downstream would pull Hank in too, and we both would drown. Hank spread-eagled himself on the bank, desperately trying to resist the pull of the rope, but he was dragged relentlessly to the edge. I was helpless, one moment smashed against the rocks on the river bottom, then forced up, gasping for air.

I smashed into the far bank seconds before Hank was dragged the final few feet into the river. Lying on the hard gravel, battered and gasping, shaking from the cold, I felt the sting of a hundred cuts and bruises, but no bones were broken. My teammates patched me up, got some hot tea into me and wrapped me in dry blankets.

We then drove 18 miles to the hotel, heading for the steaks that Hank and I had almost died for.

When I think now of those desperate seconds in that roaring flood, it's easy to dismiss our decision to cross the river at flood stage as the foolish action of youth, but I've found that gray hair is no guarantee against making stupid decisions. Still—what if, standing on that far bank, thinking of those steaks, we'd more carefully assessed the dangers and considered what we were about to do?

To be absolutely honest, we were so impatient that afternoon and so convinced that we were invincible, we might still have gone ahead. But the hard facts remain: two of us came within a hair's-breadth of dying for a risk that was totally avoidable and whose benefits were minimal. Yes, it was exciting. *But the whole rest of my life might not have happened because of that one rash move.* No way was it worth missing out on all that's happened since—it was stupid. We'd just made this dangerous, world-class first ascent, avoiding deadly avalanches only because we'd spent days carefully plotting their courses and the times of the day when they were most likely to fall. Now, after all that careful planning to keep ourselves alive on the mountain, we were coming back to acclaim—that climb made mountaineering history—and we almost threw it all away fording a river that anyone could have waded across at low water. Dumb. Really dumb.

---

### What's the point?
There are enough dangers in life you can't avoid.
When you *do* have a choice, avoid stupid risks
that gain you nothing of value.

---

In the years since surviving that decision, I've had to make a lot of choices—in Libya, in Vietnam, at the UN, at the Giraffe Project, and in my personal life. Some of my decisions were bad ones and some of them were good, but along the way I've developed some guidance that helps me make better choices. Here's the advice I wish I'd used, standing on the bank of a river, wondering whether or not to risk my life for a steak ~

~ *Think ahead.* Anticipate decisions you might have to make, weighing your options in advance. This reduces the pressures on you when the time comes, either by helping you make a more informed choice, or by prompting early actions that make a later decision easier, or even unnecessary.

> *For the Lake McChubb group, they start thinking well in advance about whether or not they want a VIP to attend their kick-off event. They assess the possible delays this might cause and the media benefits that it might bring. When the time comes to make the decision, they've already done some sound thinking that helps them choose wisely.*

On the McKinley trip, we could have easily avoided that whole terrible decision if we'd just timed our trip to arrive at the river at low water.

~ *Take a deep breath.* Take a *couple* deep breaths. The calmer you are, the better you'll do. When we got to the river, if we'd stopped to brew that tea *before* making our decision, it might have changed everything.

~ *Come up with as many options as you can.* Conventional thinking often works well. The conventional option for us on the bank of the McKinley would have been waiting for low water, definitely the best move. But sometimes the best options might be those that aren't so obvious. A good rule of thumb—whether you've got five minutes or five days to make a decision—is always allow some time to look past conventional options, things that are obvious or that you've done before or seen others do. Go beyond relying on advice from the same friends and trusting the same guides. Ask yourself—What's a way to solve this problem that's different from the usual solutions?

On a whale-watching trip a few years ago—in Alaska again— three of us were out in a Zodiac—a light rubber boat powered by an outboard motor. When a whale surfaced right in front of us, the guy in the stern cut the throttle too fast and the little boat took on so much water it began to sink. We had seconds to bail it out, or we'd be swimming in ice water. We looked for a bailing can. There was none. What else would hold water? Hands were too small. Hats were too porous. But we were all wearing rubber boots. Instant, off-the-wall solution: each of us pulled off a boot and bailed like crazy. The boat was soon safe again, and all it cost was three cold feet.

> On the Lake McChubb project, let's say that a class of 6<sup>th</sup>-graders from a nearby middle school offers to help. The 6<sup>th</sup>-graders are enthusiastic, but they don't have skills or experience and they may require a lot of supervising that the McChubb group doesn't want to do. The obvious options the group sees are: accept the offer or turn it

*down. But when they push past the obvious, they come up with a third option: pair the 6th-graders with seniors they can recruit from a nearby home for retirees, and put the pairs in charge of the trash cleanup and bench painting.*

~ *Get the best information you can on each option.* In the time you've got, think of all the pros and cons you can for each option. List them on paper if you can. If not, then just do it in your head. You don't have to take a clipboard with you every time you have to make a decision; it's a way of *thinking* that I'm suggesting. The process can look complicated at first, but as you get more experienced with it, it flows quickly and easily.

Here's how the pros and cons look for the decision the Lake McChubb group has to make about the 6th-graders:

OPTION 1: Accept the offer.

PROS

* Could be a good source of help, especially on some of the routine jobs.

* Could inspire the 6th-graders to take on projects of their own.

* Could get some middle school parents involved, who could donate time or money.

CONS

* 6th-graders could be pretty out-of-control; working with them could be more trouble than it's worth.

OPTION 2: Tell them no

PROS:

* Avoids hassle of dealing with 6th-graders.

CONS:

* Passes up a chance for extra hands, and for involving middle school parents.

* Will disappoint some of the 6th-graders.

OPTION 3: Accept the offer, pair the 6th-graders with seniors and assign them to cleanup and bench painting.

PROS:

* Doubles the amount of extra help.

✱ *Requires little supervision from original group.*
✱ *Could be an enjoyable "grandparents" experience.*
*CONS:*
✱ *We have to recruit the retirees.*

~ **Weigh the pros and cons of each option.** If you see that the cons of any option outweigh the pros, then eliminate that option from further consideration—unless all the other options are even worse. At the McKinley River, the option of crossing immediately had a positive possibility (the steak dinner) and a negative one (death). We should have seen that the cons massively outweighed the pros for this option.

~ **Choose.** Out of the options whose pros are greater than their cons, pick the one whose pros *most* outweigh its cons. Then check to make sure it fits with your vision of the results you want. If it doesn't, reexamine your options or change your vision. The option you choose and your vision have to be in sync.

> *The Lake McChubb group tosses out Option 2, because they decide its cons outweigh its pros. They pick Option 3 over Option 1 because they think that the "grandparenting" experience would be fun for the kids and for the elders, and they're confident they can enlist the support of the retirees. As a final step, they check Option 3 to make sure it fits with their Vision Statement:*
>
> *The levels of contaminants in the lake are dropping significantly. People are using the cleaner lake with confidence again—people are swimming and fishing, seniors are sitting on benches and talking, parents are tending babies and playing with older kids... Nobody in the area is using toxic chemicals—everybody is taking responsibility for keeping the lake and the lakeshore clean. People from other parts of the city are coming by and talking about cleaning up pollution problems where they live.*
>
> *They see that involving the retirees and the sixth-graders fits the vision. So it's a go.*

~ **Reflect.** Step back for a moment and take a look at what you've decided to do. You've come to the most rational choice, but does it *feel* right? If it doesn't, try to figure out why. Review your options and check your assumptions about pros and cons. Maybe there are options you've missed. Spend enough time to identify the source of your unease. You may confirm that your decision is right, despite your feeling. Or you may change your decision.

~ *Follow through.* Once your decision is made, put it into action.

~ *Have no regrets.* There's no such thing as a perfect decision. You do the best you can, with the information you've got. Learn from both your successes and your failures to improve your decision-making next time around.

## Taking Responsibility

✔ Being responsible is a powerful way to create positive change. But for that to happen, you have to expand the concept of being responsible to cover not just your behavior, but your *attitudes* as well.

✔ Our behavior and attitudes always affect the people and events around us, whether we see that or not and whether we like it or not. So it just makes sense for us to be more conscious of both.

✔ Part of accepting this broader definition of responsibility is learning to sweat the small stuff.

✔ Take responsibility for the effects of your communications, especially if the people you're talking to are not your age or from the same background.

✔ Don't send mixed messages—watch for inconsistencies between your words and your tone of voice, gestures and expressions.

✔ Know that you'll never see all the effects of being responsible.

✔ Taking responsibility matters. History is full of people who were responsible, and who made a difference despite the odds.

## Making Decisions

✔ Avoid stupid risks that gain you nothing of value.

✔ Consider this decision-making strategy:

~ ***Think ahead.*** Anticipate decisions you might have to make, then weigh your options in advance.

~ ***Take a deep breath.*** The calmer you are, the better you'll do.

~ ***Come up with as many options as you can***, *including some unconventional ones.*

~ *Get the best information you can on each option* in the time you've got. Find all the pros you can see for each option—then all the cons.

~ *Weigh the pros and cons of each option.*

~ *Choose.* Out of the options whose pros are greater than their cons, pick the one whose pros *most* outweigh its cons. Then check to make sure it fits with your vision.

~ *Reflect.* You've come to the most *rational* choice, but does it *feel* right? If it doesn't, try to figure out why.

~ *Follow through.*

~ *Have no regrets.* There's no such thing as a perfect decision. You do the best you can, with the information you've got.

**From the Giraffe Project's quote cache, some words of wisdom that apply to taking responsibility ~**

*Not until we can refuse to take without giving, can we create a society in which the chief activity is the common welfare.* —Helen Keller

*It is not fair to ask of others what you are not willing to do yourself.* —Eleanor Roosevelt

*Perseverance is a great element of success. If you only knock long enough and loud enough at the gate, you are sure to wake up somebody.* —Longfellow

*I find that if I'm thinking too much of my own problems and the fact that at times things are not just like I want them to be, I don't make any progress at all. But if I look around and see what I can do, and go on with that, then I move on.* —Rosa Parks

*Human beings must be judged by the challenges they define for themselves.* —Norman Cousins

*Technology enables us to do almost anything we can imagine, but we are gradually losing track of what is worth doing.* —Willis Harmon

*You may be disappointed if you fail, but you are doomed if you don't try.* —Beverly Sills

*When you stop giving and offering something to the rest of the world, it's time to turn out the lights.* —George Burns

*One can never pay in gratitude; one can only pay 'in kind' somewhere else in life.* —Anne Morrow Lindbergh

*Most of the things worth doing in the world had been declared impossible before they were done.* —Louis Brandeis

*If you don't make mistakes, you aren't really trying.* —Coleman Hawkins

# CHAPTER EIGHT

# How to Get Your Message Out— The Secrets of Good PR

This chapter is about creating good PR (public relations) for your project by using media. By "media" I mean primarily public media such as newspapers, television and radio. But there's also media that you can create yourself—speeches, Websites, flyers, brochures, posters and newsletters. All media act like megaphones: they amplify your message and get it to lots of people at once.

Why would you *want* to tell people what you're doing? After all, there's a tradition that says all good works should be anonymous.

The Giraffe Project ignores that tradition because we want good actions to multiply—and a powerful way to get them to do that is to use the incredible outreach of modern media. One of our favorite quotes is from La Rochefoucauld:

*Nothing is so contagious as an example.*
*We never do great good or great evil*
*without bringing about more of the same*
*on the part of others.*

In other words, telling the story of your project through media can prompt others to follow your example. At the Giraffe Project, we tell the stories of people sticking their necks out for the common good, not to make these Giraffes look good, but to show other people what *they* could do.

A second reason for telling your story is a practical one—the more people know about your project, the more support you'll attract, such as volunteers and money.

Finally, if your project involves public education—that is, you want people to change their attitude or behavior in some way— using media is a crucial way to get your idea across.

Much as we encourage you to go public, we also warn that being on television or in the newspaper can be pretty disorienting for anybody, young or old. Keep your cool—stay focused on your mission. Remember that good PR is *not* about making you or the people in your group look good. Your primary motive should be to communicate your vision and your message—inspiring others to support your project, to replicate it in their areas, and to take on other challenges important to *them.* If you impress your friends or make the adults in your life happy too, that's great. But if *that's* your primary motive, it'll show through, and you'll be less credible as a spokesperson.

### Creating a Media Strategy

Media coverage doesn't happen magically, so don't think that just because what you're doing is incredibly great that public media will hear about it and do a story on it. Sometimes that can happen—a curious reporter may track you down and the next thing you know the project's in the paper and on TV. But that's not usually the way it works. Stories don't just appear on TV and in newspapers— somebody alerted the stations or papers—so you'll probably have to make some moves to get media to tell your story.

*Media coverage doesn't happen magically.*

Having a well-thought-out media strategy as part of your action plan will not only bring your project to the attention of the media, it will also keep your messages focused and coordinated with each other, and consistent with your overall vision and action plan. Having a media strategy and keeping it in mind will increase your confidence in dealing with media, and make it less likely you'll be pulled off mission by the stress and chaos that often accompany broadcast or print coverage.

If you *don't* have a media strategy you'll lose opportunities to get the word out. And having a media strategy increases the chances reporters or editors will get your story right—though even the best work on your part is no guarantee they won't make some mistakes.

The answers to these basic questions form your strategy ~

~ Whom do you want to reach?

~ What do you want to tell them?

~ When do you need them to know?

~ What actions in this project will make good stories?

~ What kinds of media will work best for your project?

~ What kinds of printed materials do you need to create?

*The Lake McChubb group's strategy coordinates several media efforts aimed at convincing the public that the lake can be made healthy and beautiful, and that minimizing use of toxic house and garden chemicals is a vital step. The group needs public support as soon as possible, so they create a kick-off event in which the Mayor leads a short ceremony at the lake shore. Their aim is to get a story on the kick-off in the local newspaper and, because they have a lot of interesting visuals, they're also trying for the evening television news. Utilizing other media, they are putting up posters all over the community, inviting people to the kick-off and to a series of presentations to local citizens' groups. They will also publish a simple brochure and get it to every household in the area. Every printed piece they create will include the URL address for a Website that will contain much more information on their project.*

## Dealing with Public Media

*Events and actions can attract media.* Think of events or actions that will happen in the course of your project that you think would be especially interesting to people—that's what the media will be most likely to cover.

Especially if you need early public support for your project, you could invite media to a kick-off event that communicates your vision and enthusiasm. Getting a VIP to be part of a kick-off event can attract media (but the invitation has to go out weeks in advance). The attraction works both ways: VIPs will be more likely to come to your event if they know media are invited.

You can also invite media to cover your project when it's underway, pegged to a turning point such as planting the 100th tree or welcoming the 50th kid into your tutoring program. Completion events like ribbon-cuttings and celebrations are another possibility; even though media coverage of these events is too late to help *your* project, it can inspire others to replicate what you're doing or start other kinds of projects.

All media have deadlines. If you want coverage for a particular date and time, check cut-off times with any media whose coverage you want. For a morning newspaper, the deadline is probably midnight the night before. For afternoon papers, it's anywhere from 8 AM to noon. For weeklies, it might be 24 hours in advance. For television, if they're not going live, the cameras have to finish at least 2 hours before air time.

*For good photos or footage, something visual has to be going on.*

To get good newspaper photographs or television footage, something visual has to be going on—people talking on phones or reading won't attract cameras. Well before a photographer or a TV cameraperson arrives, consider what they will see. A TV camera roams around shooting the "B-roll" ("A-roll" is the main event, the key interviews; B-roll is the visuals that run under the reporter's voice, setting the mood and giving a visual background to the story.) Clean up visually distracting clutter and then strategically place posters or pictures or other visuals that will help you get your message across. While the best reporters and camera people won't need much guidance, it's still a good idea to point out your visuals when they arrive. You'll be helping them do a good job quickly.

We're interviewed often at the Giraffe Project office. So we have a 4x4-foot collage of newspaper stories about Giraffes, a large wall map with pins showing where we've found Giraffes, giraffe posters, and a life-size *papier-mâché* giraffe. Cameras head for these visuals every time.

*The Lake McChubb group has invited the Mayor to speak at a short kick-off ceremony at the lake shore, after which he will demonstrate a new mulching mower that eliminates the need for chemical lawn fertilizers. They'll also make some large charts showing how the levels of pollution in the lake have risen over the last 20 years. The lawnmower demonstration should be a great attention grabber and the charts will portray the problem for the cameras much more powerfully than words. The group also identifies a part of the lake where there is a lot of trash on the shoreline and scum on the water—a shot of that will help dramatize the problem.*

The McChubb group's kick-off event includes a VIP (the Mayor) and an interesting action (the lawnmower demo). The group's charts, and a visit to the area with the trash and scum, will provide good "B-roll."

***Writing Press Releases.*** A press release is written information sent to the editors of newspapers or to program directors of television and radio stations. It can invite media to cover an event and/or to do a story based on what's in the release. Sending a release is no guarantee that media will respond—there are many competing stories and yours may well get ignored. But if you *don't* send a release, the media definitely won't know what you're doing.

*Sending a release is no guarantee that media will respond.*

Press releases are usually written with the most important information first and the least important last. This allows editors to cut the piece from the bottom up if they need to shorten the story, without picking through the paragraphs. Your task is to make the editor's job as easy as possible, which increases the chances of the release being used. To write a good release ~

~ Keep it short; one page is best.

~ Give the important facts, without exaggerating.

~ Confine opinions to quotes by individuals, giving their names and titles.

~ Double-space it, setting wide margins on the sides for editors to write in.

~ Include a release date and at least one name and number that reporters can call for more information.

~ Enclose background materials—but just a few, not pounds of them.

The next page is a sample press release about the launch of the McChubb project. It's written to send *prior* to an event to encourage media people to come and see it for themselves. A press release can also be sent *after* an event, describing what happened.

*(date)*

*For Immediate Release*

**Mayor to Kick Off McChubb Cleanup, A Project by Local Students**

*Mayor Frank Jones will help launch a student-led project to clean up Lake McChubb Saturday, March 7 at 10 AM at the public park on the lake's north shore.*

*City studies show that levels of toxic chemicals in Lake McChubb began to rise 20 years ago; the Health Department has announced that any increase will lead to a ban on swimming and fishing. While local use of household and garden chemicals was identified in a 1998 study by the Department as a major factor in this pollution, no concerted effort has ever been made to correct the situation.*

*Now 30 students at Lincoln High School have announced that they will start such an effort. Project spokesperson Kate Wright says that the students have designed a campaign to inform local residents about alternatives to using toxic chemicals in their homes and on their lawns, and have already enlisted the support of several nurseries and hardware stores. At Saturday's event, Mayor Jones will demonstrate a new mulching mower that is one way to eliminate the need for chemical lawn fertilizers.*

*Wright says that the students' plan includes cleaning up debris on the lake front and repainting the park benches. This part of the work will be done by teams made up of volunteers from the 6th grade at Holly Elementary and residents of the Mt. Zion Baptist Retirement Home.*

*Developments in the project can be tracked on the project's Website:*
*<http://www.mcchubb/lincolnhs.edu>*

*Susan Harrison, Principal at Lincoln High, says she's been impressed by the students' commitment. "They're tackling this challenge in a very constructive way," she said. "I hope the community will support them in reviving the lake."*

*The cleanup is part of the Giraffe Heroes Program, an initiative of the Giraffe Project, a national nonprofit that moves people to "stick their necks out for the common good."*

*— END —*

*For more information call: Kendra Watkins (phone number)*

It's a good idea to follow up a press release with a phone call. If you call, add a piece of new information that wasn't in the release, as a way of building more interest in your story.

Many television stations use *video* press releases. If your group has the skills and equipment, call or email local stations and ask about their policies and standards for such footage.

***Doing Interviews.*** A newspaper or a broadcast station may respond to your press release by assigning a reporter to interview you about it.

Assume that reporters will be sympathetic to a community service project, and that they'll want to work with you to tell the story in an interesting and positive way. They know they need your help to do that. Nevertheless, expect them to be moving fast—most reporters are busy people and most newsrooms run on crowded, high-pressure schedules. You'll do fine if you remember a few basic tips ~

~ **Be prepared.** Review the vision for your project, your overall plan and your media strategy before the interview. Think through this particular media opportunity and decide on the key points you want to get across.

*The key points for a Lake McChubb spokesperson are:*
* *pollution in the lake affects the whole town's quality of life*
* *a major pollution source is household and garden chemicals*
* *trash and graffiti on the lakeshore are a growing problem*
* *a big part of the solution is education; alternatives to toxic chemicals are available, and they work*
* *brief description of the group, its motives and vision*
* *key details of the group's action plan*
* *what people can do to help*
* *Website address*
* *end by returning to the vision*

If you're going to be on TV or radio, remember that broadcast time is short and a rambling interview won't be used—so practice getting your key points across in short, to-the-point sentences.

Role-play the interview with a friend, or record your key points and play them back to see if you're on the mark.

Assemble any backup information you might need for the interview, such as charts and pictures.

~ *Communicate your vision.* By now it should be sharply honed. The more clearly you're able to convey it, the better chance you have of getting the reporter—and the audience—excited about your project. You need to get all the relevant facts across, but when a reporter begins to share the excitement of your vision, she'll ask better questions and be more likely to write a story or do a voice-over that captures the excitement and importance of your project.

Be on the lookout for interviews on television or in newspapers or magazines. As you watch or read them, notice the ones that give you a lot of facts, and those that focus on someone's vision for the future, on something exciting that could be done. Note which interviews hold your attention, and why.

~ *Keep the interview on* **your** *issue.* Your reporter may well show up with interesting and relevant questions, but there's no guarantee that'll be the case. Sometimes a reporter will not have done her homework, or have any real interest in your project. She may also have several stories to do that day, and be tired or distracted. So it's important for *you* to keep the interview on course. Whether or not the reporter asks you the questions you want to answer, make sure that you get your key points across. Don't waste the time you'll have on issues that may be off the point. Here's how that works ~

> Question: "This lake cleanup is nice, but what do you think about teen violence—all those kids who are shooting up their schools?"

> Answer: "I can't speak for them, but I do know that every one of us who's working to clean up Lake McChubb feels really good

*about what we're doing, working with the community and making
a really big change that's going to last for a long time. I'd like
everyone to know how exciting this stuff can be."*

The reporter asked a question that led far from the McChubb
project; the project spokesperson politely brought the focus right
back to Lake McChubb and to serving the community.

~ *Be yourself.* Take a deep breath, remember your main points and
speak as *you.* You don't have to imitate a pro and shouldn't try—
the viewers, listeners or readers will connect with you as the person you are. Remember that most of these people will be older
than you are, so it's probably wise to avoid slang that they may
not understand. If you don't know the answer to a question, don't
pretend to be all-knowing and fake an answer. Just say you don't
know but you'll find out.

~ *Follow-up.* Find out when the story will be broadcast or printed.
*Make copies*—tape any broadcasts and clip any newspapers. Not
everybody who should see your story will see it when it runs—but
they'll see it if you send them a copy.

Keep contact information on your media allies. Send a thank-
you to every reporter who does a story. It's just good manners,
and to be practical, you might want coverage later on for another
project, and your courtesy will be remembered.

### Creating Websites, Flyers, Posters and Brochures

Consider developing a Website to describe your project, post news
and photos of your progress, ask for support, and invite comments.
Website design is beyond the scope of this book, but there are
plenty of books on the subject. Web costs can be eliminated or kept
low if you can get a server to donate the site, and if someone in your
group can design it, or you can find a pro to volunteer. Put your
Website's URL address on every piece of printed material you create
for your project, and include it in any speech or interview.

Many Giraffes honored by the Giraffe Project use Websites to build support for their causes. Students from Broad Meadows Middle School in Quincy, Massachusetts used the Web to create an international network of support for banning child slave labor, and to raise money for building a school for freed child slaves in Pakistan. Another group of students in Washington State used the Web to build global support to free Lolita, a captive orca whale.

Flyers and posters have to convey simple messages quickly and powerfully. They are visual media; the words should be minimal. Their purpose is not to explain every detail of an idea or *In visual* a position, but *to grab the viewer/reader's attention*, if only for a moment, and keep the focus on a single, simple message, such *media,* as coming to an event or not using pesticides. The trick in creating a good flyer or poster is to give just enough information, *stress* without putting in so many words that you undercut the visual power of the piece. See the two pages that follow for a good *images,* McChubb flyer and a really bad one.

Brochures also need to be visually strong, but they can contain more information, not only attracting the reader's interest *not* in the subject but also explaining positions, describing accomplishments, and ending with your requests for the reader's ac- *words.* tion. But use as few words as possible to do all that. Too many words, and tightly crowded type, undercut the power of a brochure.

Because flyers, posters and brochures depend heavily on visuals, they're good vehicles for conveying your vision. When you're designing them, start by revisiting your vision. What in that mental picture could be turned into a good graphic, that would attract and hold attention?

# Scrub McChubb
### Saturday April 14
### 9 am till dusk

Please join Lincoln High students
to make Lake McChubb
safe and beautiful again.

**Help with the cleanup.**
Come to the 8th Street dock
Bring trash bags, rakes, gloves,
and friends.

**Find out *why* the water is unsafe
and what you can do about it.**

Enjoy great snacks from
Marie's Deli & Joey's Ice Cream Shop

## PEOPLE ARE LETTING CHEMICALS POLLUTE LAKE MCCHUBB AND THROWING TRASH WE WANT YOU TO HELP US CLEAN IT UP.

Lake McChubb was a beautiful lake at one time but now the Health Department is threatening to close it to swimming and fishing because of pollution and there is litter, and cans and bottles and dead fish and paper and garbage all around the shoreline and the picnic area and it's because some people just don't seem to care. They use toxic chemicals that get into the lake and they go there and swim and camp and party and throw all their trash on the ground instead of in one of the twelve trash cans that are there.

We are the students at Lincoln High School and we are doing a project to clean up the trash and garbage that people who don't care throw all around Lake McChubb. We also want people to stop using chemicals on their lawns to kill weeds that get into the water and kill the fish and stink up the water and even make people sick.

On Sat. you can find out what you should use on your lawns and even soaps you should use in your washing machines and on your cars and trucks and the kind of mower to use and pick up the trash.

**DON'T BE LATE**

Bring your lawn tools and trash bags. We'll have snacks. And you can call Larry Davis at #443-7670

## Giving a Speech

Standing up in front of a bunch of people and giving a presentation can be frightening. I think that's because it seems to be about being judged as a person. What will people think of you—of your appearance, your intelligence, your motives, your words?

The first thing you need to know is that *you are not the point of the speech*—your message is the point. Focus on getting *that* across and on how much you want your audience to share it, and you'll lessen your concern about yourself.

Learning to speak in public is a valuable life skill; the risks and effort it takes to become a good speaker are worth it. Like anything else, speaking can become less frightening as you gain experience. If you want to build your skills as a speaker, practice. Start with presentations to small audiences of people you know and like. As you gain confidence, volunteer to address strangers. Watch experienced speakers and notice what they do. If you have access to the equipment, videotape yourself practicing and doing presentations. Learn from what you see. Invite feedback from people whose opinions you trust.

Learning to speak well doesn't mean your goal has to be bringing a thousand people to their feet, cheering. Just getting your points made without freezing up is a triumph, if you thought you could never do that.

You *can* do this. Here are some tried and true tips on how:

***Learn about the people you'll be talking to before you speak***, so you can start from where they are, saying things that will engage and hold their attention. Question people familiar with this audience. Make a few phone calls to people who will actually *be* in the audience and ask your questions directly. I find people almost always willing to help this way, because they know they're helping make my speech more relevant and interesting.

Try to find out ~

~ How familiar is this audience with the subject you're going to talk to them about? You don't want to tell them a lot of things they already know, but you also don't want to assume they know more than they do about your subject.

~ Do they have any attitudes and beliefs that might influence them to agree with you—or keep them from doing that? Someone who is advocating free needle exchanges, for example, should expect a tough audience at a conservative church. Ask people who will be there what they think about the subject of your presentation. You can also learn a lot by finding out who's spoken to this audience in the past and how people reacted to their speeches.

~ What special concerns do they have that might connect with your vision?

> One Lake McChubb speaker has found out that there will be a lot of young parents in her audience, so she decides to start her speech by talking about creating a safe place to teach their kids to swim. Another McChubb speaker has learned that his audience is elderly, longtime residents, so he plans to talk about the lake as his audience remembers it, healthy and beautiful.

**Make an outline of what you want to say**, whether you're an experienced speaker or not. Here's a useful form ~

~ *Introduce yourself and tell people why you're speaking to them.*

~ *Give a short summary of what you're about to say.*

~ *Describe the problem that concerns you/the group and suggest why your audience should care about it too.* Use enough detail to show you've done your homework, but don't put your audience to sleep with endless numbers.

> A speaker from the Lake McChubb group describes how pollution levels in the lake have been rising, and how that could lead to a ban on swimming and fishing. But he doesn't read sheets of supporting statistics; they can be on a handout for people who are interested in that level of detail.

~ *Communicate your/the group's vision for solving this problem.* Visions convey passion, and they inspire people to action. You don't have to use the word "vision"—you can just call it a "picture," but be sure to convey all the excitement and enthusiasm your group has created around its vision.

*The Lake McChubb speaker invites his audience to share his group's vision of a lake that's no longer polluted, perhaps picturing themselves and their families swimming and fishing in a clean lake.*

~ *Describe the plan for reaching your vision, and why it will work.* People are more interested in helping with a project if they know it's well thought-out and they can see that the people behind it are committed. You can convey that commitment by telling stories of your progress, including how the group chose this project and how they've overcome obstacles.

*The Lake McChubb speaker describes his group's action plan and shares a few stories of how they created it and how they are carrying it out. But the audience doesn't need or want to know the details of each step in that plan.*

~ *Explain what you need from your audience.* Tell them how the action or contribution you're seeking will help make the vision for your project a reality. Tell them how they can contribute.

*"This vision won't just happen," the Lake McChubb speaker says. "It takes a good plan, a lot of work and some money. We have the plan, but we need money to pay for printing brochures, and we need volunteers to help deliver them door-to-door; that's how we can get people to focus on reducing or stopping their use of toxic chemicals." He urges everyone in his audience to sign a pledge to reduce or eliminate their own use of toxic chemicals in their houses and gardens; he tells them that the pledge form is on a table by the door, as are volunteer sign-up sheets and envelopes for contributions.*

~ *Summarize.* Hearing a presentation is not like reading a book or magazine; listeners can't go back and look up a point they missed. So recap your main points shortly before you end. If there are many points, and/or a lot of technical data, hand out supporting materials or have them on display.

~ *Q & A.* If there's time to answer questions after your presentation, offer to do so. Q & A's are a good opportunity to clear up anything your audience may not have understood, and to reinforce your important points. Don't worry about being asked questions you can't answer—if you don't know, say so. You can always offer to get back to the questioner when you do have the information.

## Things to Remember When You Give a Speech

**1** *Connect with the people in your audience.* Audiences are more likely to follow the lead of speakers they can connect to and the more connected you feel to *them*, the more confident you'll be. Don't see an audience as a roomful of opinions to be swayed, but as *people* who want to do something meaningful with their lives as much as you do. Assume they're good people and that your information and vision can be of real benefit to them. If you bring this attitude to your speech, your audience will pick it up, and it will help link them to you and your message.

My method is to pick out a few people in the audience and focus on them as if I were speaking to them alone. I can feel the links this creates, and that adds to my confidence that I can reach others—even that guy reading the newspaper in the sixth row.

**2** *Be yourself.* Audiences quickly sense faking or posturing or pretending. Just be who you are. If you're a fifteen-year-old girl who's never made a speech before, be that girl—don't try to imitate some slick anchorwoman.

**3** *Speak from your heart as well as your head.* Don't be afraid to express your feelings in a speech—especially in telling personal stories—and to draw out the feelings of people in your audience with questions they can answer silently.

> *A Lake McChubb speaker says, "My dad told me about the lake he remembers. When he grew up here, the lake was really clean and nobody was afraid to swim in it. I really feel sad that it's polluted now. I bet I'm not the only one here who feels that way..."*

**4** *Read as little as possible of your speech and make your points using personal stories.*

> *In describing community attitudes, the Lake McChubb speaker talks about her experiences of distributing brochures door-to-door—she just*

*talks, she doesn't read. She describes visits when people listened to her—and visits when they didn't. She relates what her group learned about community attitudes toward the lake from both kinds of experiences.*

5 *Don't use a lot of overhead projections, computer-assisted graphics, or charts.* They *can* be great for getting information across, but novice speakers tend to use too many, so the audience will look at the pictures and not at the speaker. It's more important for the audience to get the message from *you*, not the graphics. It's *your* vision and *your* enthusiasm that's going to bring them around, not the pictures.

6 *Respect your audience* in your tone, style and dress. If any of these things are too different from what your audience is comfortable with, it can and probably will keep them from hearing you. If you have doubts about what's appropriate, ask someone who's been there.

I know a very smart political activist who refuses to clean up or comb his hair before he speaks at government hearings; to him, it's a matter of principle. Fine, that's his right. But I don't have much patience when this same guy complains that the officials don't want to listen to him. The officials interpret his "style" as a lack of respect for them—and they're right.

7 *Expect to succeed.* Everybody knows that giving a speech can be frightening. Whether they show it or not, your audience will respect you for having the courage to be up there. Most of them will be more than willing to cut you some slack. Still, experienced speakers know that you can't please everybody every time. When I've given speeches, I've had people in the same audience tell me that I both spoke too long and not long enough, and that the same joke was wonderfully funny and that it fell flat. If you get your message and your vision across as well as you can—that's a success.

✔ Getting your project into the media can prompt others to follow your example, attract support for your project, and help you educate people about your issue.

✔ Good PR is about those goals, not about making you or the people in your group famous.

✔ A well-thought-out media strategy will not only achieve those goals, it will also keep your messages focused and consistent with your overall vision and action plan. The answers to these questions form your media strategy ~
  ~ Whom do you want to reach?
  ~ What do you want to tell them?
  ~ When do they need to know?
  ~ What actions in the project will make good stories?
  ~ What kinds of media will work best for the project?
  ~ What kinds of printed materials do you need to create?

✔ Think of interesting actions that will happen in the course of your project—that's what media will be most likely to cover.

✔ A press release is written information sent to the editors of newspapers or to program directors of television and radio stations. A release can invite them to cover an event and/or do a story based on the release.

✔ In doing interviews, assume that reporters will be sympathetic to a community service project, and that they'll want to tell the story in a positive way, but don't leave all the work to the interviewer.
  ~ *Be prepared.* Review the vision for your project, your overall plan and your media strategy. Decide on the key points you want to get across.
  ~ *Communicate your vision.*
  ~ *Keep the interview on* your *issue,* whether or not the reporter asks you the questions you expect.

~ *Be yourself.* Take a deep breath, remember your main points and speak as *you.*

✔ Consider developing a Website to describe your project, post news of your progress, ask for support, and invite comments.

✔ Good flyers, posters and brochures convey simple messages quickly and powerfully. They are visual media so they're good vehicles for conveying your vision.

✔ You *can* give a speech. Just remember that:
- *You are not the point*—your message is the point. Focus on getting *that* across and you'll lower the pressure on yourself.
- *Learn in advance about the people you'll be talking to,* so you can start from where they are, saying things that will get and hold their attention.
- *Make an outline of what you want to say,* using this form ~
    - ~ Introduce yourself and tell people why you're there.
    - ~ Give a short summary of what you're about to say.
    - ~ Describe the issue or problem that concerns you / the group and suggest why your audience should care about it too.
    - ~ Communicate the vision for solving this problem.
    - ~ Describe your / the group's plan for tackling this issue and reaching your vision. Explain why your plan will work.
    - ~ Explain what you need from your audience.
    - ~ Summarize.

When you give your speech ~
1. *Connect with the people in your audience.*
2. *Be yourself.* Audiences quickly sense faking or posturing.
3. *Speak from your heart as well as your head.*
4. *Read as little as possible of your speech and make your points using stories and examples.*
5. *Don't use a lot of overhead projections, computer-assisted graphics or charts.*
6. *Respect your audience in your tone, style and dress.*
7. *Expect to succeed.*

# CHAPTER NINE

# Finding Common Ground

*Planning for an event goes badly because the two people who are supposed to lead it can't stand each other...*

*A meeting drags on because someone insists on getting his way on every point...*

*Nasty gossip is floating around about you—spread by somebody who says you insulted him two months ago...*

*A service project comes to a halt when local homeowners complain that you're "meddling" in their neighborhood...*

*You're in a social group whose members avoid the people in another group—who don't think much of you either...*

This chapter is about dealing effectively with conflicts, wherever and whenever you find them. The tips here are for you, but if you're part of a group that's facing conflict, it's important that your whole group consider them too. It's hard to create a dialogue if others in your group think the only way to deal with conflict is to fight until they "win."

Much of the information comes from my own experiences. Some of those were big deals, like face-offs with the Soviets when I was in the Foreign Service, or environmental battles in the Pacific Northwest. But most of them were much smaller and more personal, including difficulties within my own community and my own family.

The first thing I learned about conflicts is that, nine times out of ten, whenever people get stuck, it's not because they're not smart enough to figure out solutions. *It's because they can't get through their own emotional baggage to work things out.* That's true everywhere, from the Balkans to your backyard.

 Think of conflicts you've been in, at home, at school, at work—anywhere. Replay the worst ones in your mind. Can you think of any that continued because people weren't smart enough to solve them? Can you think of any that continued because one or both sides were stuck in emotions they couldn't get past?

I also learned that the best way to resolve conflicts is *not* to try to outwit or overpower the people who are giving you grief. Winning by making somebody lose usually creates losers on all sides—your "victory" causes festering resentments that undermine relationships and cause the same conflict to surface again and again, sometimes in new forms.

 Have you ever been involved in a conflict that seemed to go on forever, with every minor "victory" by one side ratcheting up the conflict one more notch? If you have, what happened? How did it end? *Did* it end?

There are better options than creating winners and losers. It's possible to create *real* solutions to conflicts—solutions that will last because everyone is truly satisfied with them. The steps on the following pages will help you deal with any conflict. They're simple in concept but not simple to implement, because they call for high levels of compassion, courage and self-control.

These are guidelines—assume you'll have to improvise. Some of the steps described below may not be needed in the situation you're in, or you may need to apply them in some creative new combination of your own.

**Here are the steps:**

1 Handle your "inside stuff."

2 Look for stereotypes and negative judgments you may have of people who oppose you.

3 Look beneath the "waterline."

4 Build trust.

5 Look for easy fixes.

6 Confirm the issues that are still in conflict.

7 Help people create a shared vision.

8 Build an agreement on the common ground you find.

9 Commit to carrying out the agreement.

**1 Handle your "inside stuff."** You're in charge of your reactions to other people, no matter what the provocation. An out-of-control reaction from you increases the provoker's control. Don't blame a mean teacher or a bratty little brother for pushing you into losing your cool, no matter how bad their behavior might be. Lashing out is the "easy" response to conflict, and it will just make things worse. Not taking the easy way is tough—but there's a lot to be said for being in charge of yourself instead of letting others jerk you around.

How do you feel when someone else's actions or words make you lose your temper or your self-confidence?

**2 Look for stereotypes and negative judgments you may have of people who oppose you.** Hanging on to your judgments gives the other person no chance to improve, and may actually reinforce their negative behavior—if you're convinced that someone you know will always lie, and he knows that, what incentive does he have to be truthful? By giving others the benefit of the doubt, at least initially, you give them room to rise to their best. If they fail to do that, you'll have to adopt a more defensive approach. But if they respond positively, it can be a major breakthrough for ending a conflict.

And don't forget that others may be acting on negative judgments they have of *you*. By suspending your judgments, you give them a model for reevaluating their assessments of you.

 Think of negative judgments you have of people you've had conflicts with. Now think of negative judgments they might have of you. What effect have these judgments had on finding good solutions?

◆••••••••••••••••••••••••••••••••••••••••••••••••••◆

**3 Look beneath the waterline.** Have you ever been in a conflict and sensed that something else was going on—something very important to that conflict—that nobody was talking about? Conflicts are never what they appear to be. Those that you see are like the tips of icebergs. Think of the *Titanic*. The dangerous part of an iceberg is not the 1/8 you can see; it's the 7/8 you can't. The top of the iceberg is that part of a conflict people talk about openly. But the real problems are often deeper, below the waterline, involving feelings people *don't* talk about and may not even realize are there.

It could be a hidden agenda. A largely white community may try to block a low-income housing project by arguing it will lower their property values—but the real issue might be racism; they think all the new residents will be people of color, and they don't want them in their neighborhood.

A key buried issue is often people's fear of change, of leaving the security of what's known to risk doing something new.

The toughest issues are those buried deep in the iceberg— sensitive factors like fear and lack of self-esteem. This is the kind of stuff that can feed on people for years, underlie prejudices like racism, and make people defensive, short-tempered and combative.

It's not easy to get at stuff like this, let alone deal with it, in part because none of us is perfect and what you think you see in someone else's iceberg may only be a prejudice or stereotype of your own. Still, the more aware you are of hidden issues—including your own—the better chance you'll have to resolve conflicts that flow from those issues.

*Getting to the issues below the waterline will help you solve the real problem.* Discovering that racist attitudes are behind a community's opposition to low-income housing won't end the racism, but it *will* keep the promoters of that housing from basing their whole case on surface arguments, such as property values, and it *will* help them develop an approach that takes the community's deeper attitudes into account. They could bring people from the community to a neighborhood meeting in a successful low-income housing development they've already built. There, the visitors could see for themselves not only that many races are represented in low-income housing, but that multiethnic neighborhoods can have a positive, respectful civic life.

*Understanding the below-the-waterline issues will help you be more constructive with people.* If you see that someone cringes every time there's a loud disagreement in your group, you might be careful in how you speak to her. But you're likely to be even more understanding if you know that her reactions were formed from being raised in an abusive family.

*Sensitive, caring actions can break up emotional logjams.*

If there's someone in your group who seems to oppose everything the group wants to do, perhaps you sense that it's a lack of self-confidence that makes him so contrary and obstinate. If that's the case, go out of your way to acknowledge the contributions this person's already made, to make sure he gets at least his share of public credit, and to ask for his opinion often.

Sensitive, caring actions at this level in the iceberg *can* break up emotional logjams. Obviously you can't be phony about any of this—you have to mean it or it'll backfire.

*Addressing buried issues will help you avoid compromise "solutions" that don't solve the problem.* The iceberg is why conventional compromises rarely work to resolve a conflict: too often they fail to deal with the *real* issues people are fighting about, which may be deeply buried. Especially if the compromise is designed by an outside party, "splitting the difference" is usually just an arbitrary way to shut people up, a time-out from win/lose fighting. The conflict returns whenever one side or the other sees an advantage in restarting it.

A single mom comes home late after work. She's too tired to cook so she sends out for pizza. Her two boys eat most of it—until there's just one slice left. The older brother says he's entitled to it because he's older. The little brother claims that he's already had one less slice and that the one remaining is rightfully his. A fight erupts. To gain some peace, the mother divides the remaining piece down the center and gives each brother half. Each boy bolts down his half, but the anger between them doesn't stop. An hour later they're screaming at each other about choosing a TV program.

The real problem isn't the pizza and it's not the television. What the boys are really fighting for is more of their mother's attention; each thinks that getting his way on pizza or TV could mean he's the favored one. The mother needs to see the iceberg in this conflict—and deal with the real issue.

Have you ever been in a conflict in which someone in authority enforced a compromise that split the difference between you and the person you were fighting with? What was the result? Was the conflict really solved?

◆•••••••••••••••••••••••••••••••••••••••••••••••••••••◆

---

## What's the point?
Applying the iceberg concept
to conflicts can help you find solutions that will last
because they deal with the *real cause* of the conflict.

---

Think of a conflict you've been involved in. Now look at it as an iceberg. What was going on beneath the waterline of the person with whom you had the conflict? What was going on beneath your own waterline?

**4** **Build trust.** When people trust each other they become less defensive, more honest—and much more able to solve a conflict. Trust can defuse anger, fear and resentment. Trust can open the possibility of real dialogue so that people, including you, can see *underneath* the apparent conflict—go deeper into the iceberg—to deal with what the conflict is really about.

I'm not talking about the kind of trust you'd need to tell someone your deepest secrets. I'm talking about the trust that says, "OK, we disagree. But I think you're speaking honestly, that you'll keep your word, and that you'd like to do the right thing."

> Initially, the students in the Lake McChubb group and some of the homeowners around the lake didn't know or trust each other, so there were some ugly judgments on both sides. But as the students and homeowners met and discussed the issue, each side got less defensive because they saw that their judgments were exaggerated, untrue, and/or balanced by positive qualities. Discussions became more honest as each side trusted the other enough to say what was on their minds.

Think of a conflict in which you've trusted a person on the other side, even though you disagreed with him. Now think of another conflict in which there was no trust anywhere. How did trusting, or not trusting, affect your actions?

Building trust can *prevent* conflicts as well as help resolve them. If you see a conflict coming, sometimes the best move is to head *towards* opponents, not in the other direction. I understand how hard this can be, but you can often defuse potential conflicts by building trust with the people you're likely to tangle with. The more trust that's established early on, the more flexibility, patience and self-control all of you will show if and when your positions do clash later on.

"Trust? Trust *them?!!*" There's a choice to be made here. You can deal with conflict the way most people do—by either running from it or by launching some negative behavior of your own, and then watching things spiral out of control. Or you can build trust. I guarantee you that building trust will consistently resolve conflicts better than running away or duking it out.

*Building trust involves being open.* The first step in building trust with an opponent, or potential opponent, often is to find nonthreatening ways to talk, perhaps by sharing personal stories and experiences that have nothing to do with the conflict. You'll probably have to go first—reaching out like this is not standard procedure. Be as open and informal as you can, so that others will be encouraged to respond in kind. Look for common threads in personal interests and experiences. As people relax, negative judgments fade and communication becomes easier; people begin to feel safe enough to be open in ways they wouldn't have risked before. As some trust develops, you can begin to nudge the conversation towards more sensitive issues. This may take time, so be patient.

*Most people either run from conflict or fight it out.*

I was once on a three-person committee in my county to make recommendations on wetlands protection. I represented the environmentalists. The county Planning Director represented the government and a development expert represented the real estate interests. We had never agreed on anything. But instead of starting from there, we spent some time getting to know each other as people. The only common ground we could find initially was sports, so in the beginning of a process that went on for six weeks, we talked about sports a lot, from Little League to the NFL. Those conversations relaxed us, established some common interests, and let us get to know each other in a context outside the conflict. As we came to see each other as likable, understandable people, we listened more respectfully to each other's ideas, not just on the Seahawks but also on wetlands. That was quite different from our previous run-ins. We started to trust each other, acknowledging good points in each other's positions and looking for solutions we could all accept. We came to an agreement on wetlands that satisfied all sides. It wouldn't have happened if we'd slugged it out, seeing each other as "the bad guy."

*Build trust through caring and respect.* By caring I mean the active compassion described in Chapter Four—putting yourself in somebody else's shoes. By respect I mean respect for other people as human beings—their backgrounds, needs, outlooks and styles, even if any or all of these make you uncomfortable. This Giraffe did it right ~

John Hayes was raised in Aspen, Colorado, where he learned to love the land. Over time he became dismayed at the unplanned and uncontrolled development that was spoiling the area and began looking for a place in the world that was as special as Aspen had been when he was a boy. He discovered the Methow Valley in Washington State and moved there in the 1970's. Soon, however, he saw ugly, unplanned development threatening to destroy that paradise too. He vowed not to let that happen.

What he's done since for wildlife, water conservation and the protection of open space in the Methow Valley has been extraordinary. He started a nonprofit corporation to preserve open space and wildlife habitat in the valley. He designed and built a 16-mile community trail system that links cross-country ski trails with backcountry trails and service facilities. He implemented a new approach to land use that preserves more than 90% of the land as open space for scenic, wildlife and agricultural use. He's gotten water conservation standards written into county rules, convinced owners to hide their building sites in the trees and has worked closely with natural resources agencies to protect wildlife areas.

Hayes' success in creating workable solutions to very tough problems and age-old conflicts comes from more than hard work; it's come from bringing people who often are in conflict—cattle ranchers, Native Americans, environmentalists, local and state bureaucrats and politicians, corporations and land developers.

The trail project, for example, required that Hayes convince owners of 16 miles of land to give up very valuable strips of land through their properties. If even one landowner had said no, the project would have been blocked.

Part of Hayes' success in bringing people together has been his ability to convey a vision for preserving the valley. He's become the "land preacher," and through his leadership has raised the consciousness of everyone involved.

But perhaps most important has been Hayes' ability to earn the trust of virtually all the factions in the valley, a trust created by his strong sensitivity to the feelings of the many different people that he works with. Hayes understands that bridging the distance between many opposing factions means addressing all their needs and satisfying people of very different backgrounds. He knows that takes time, caring and patience, and John Hayes has given all that to saving the Methow.

**5 Look for easy fixes.** If conflict starts, look for easy fixes—not compromises that sweep real issues under the rug, but the kind of common sense things that can be missed when people, including you, get caught up in the emotions that a conflict can generate.

> *The city agrees to support the Lake McChubb anti-pollution project by moving the public parking lot back from the lake shore. Unfortunately, they don't do their homework and they publish a plan showing the new lot in a place where users are sure to walk across private property to get to it. This puts the homeowners in an uproar. But when everybody sits down around a map, they see an easy fix—an alternative site that can be accessed along city property.*

**6 Confirm the issues that are still in conflict.** If you can't find any easy fixes, make sure everybody knows what the disagreement is about.

*Outline the differences accurately.* It's amazing how often people start to fight over stuff that's really not at issue. Ask questions until everybody's clear on exactly what the differences really are.

*Explain the rationale for your positions completely. Be open about any uncertainties or downsides you see in them, and urge others to do the same.* This advice may seem strange, but it's sound. Being open can be catching. Mutual vulnerability can increase each side's respect and trust for the other, and quickly move discussions toward solutions. If your opponent treats your openness with contempt or tries to take advantage of it, you can always put your defenses back up. But being open in this way is well worth trying. I've seen it result in major breakthroughs many times.

*Get more information if you need it.* Now that you've pinpointed the real differences that separate the sides, look for any sources of information that might shed new light on those issues.

**7 Help people create a shared vision.** With the problem defined, emotions in check, and some trust created—jump ahead to suggest a vision for a solution to the conflict that all sides can willingly accept. Call it a "picture" if that makes people more comfortable. Ask others to contribute to it. It will be a picture, not of a cleverer way to split old differences—but of an imaginative new solution that benefits everybody.

You may be surprised at how much agreement there is. Keep refining a joint vision as it emerges; the more detailed it becomes, the more it can inspire both sides to keep talking, and the better it can guide everyone to an agreement on the specific steps that will make the vision real.

> The Lake McChubb group runs into opposition from a local homeowners' association whose members are afraid that the students will push for extreme solutions, including a ban on house and garden chemicals that will take away homeowners' individual freedom to make their own decisions. The students, for their part, start out seeing many of the homeowners as selfish and shallow, not knowing or caring about the effect on the lake of the house and garden chemicals they use.

*Initial discussions between the students and the homeowners help build trust. The students' media strategy helps too. Residents see their brochures and flyers, plus a story in the newspaper and one on television. The students do a presentation to the homeowners' association and continue going door-to-door talking to residents. The homeowners see the students as more responsible than they had thought, while the students find many homeowners quite concerned and willing to make some sacrifices to lessen pollution in the lake. But a key stumbling block remains: the homeowners insist that the changes demanded by a no-toxics approach shouldn't be extreme. They aren't willing to let weeds overrun their lawns or to wear clothes that aren't clean.*

*The students rely on their research into nontoxic ways to wash clothes and cars and to care for lawns and gardens. They convince local merchants to offer substantial discounts on nontoxic products. Then they demonstrate these products to the homeowners and offer price comparisons. The homeowners listen, and propose a change in the students' vision for their project—reducing use of toxics through voluntary measures. The students had been planning to ask the city to impose a ban, but they realize that if voluntary measures worked, that would be a better, less confrontational way of reviving the lake.*

*One of the homeowners, an artist, agrees to help design "Toxics Free Zone" signs that complying houses can put on their lawns and in their windows. Meanwhile, the students continue with their presentations, visits, brochures, flyers and media coverage. They know, and the homeowners know, that if voluntary measures don't work, the next step is a ban.*

*Students and homeowners now share the same vision; the changes from the students' original vision are shown by strikeouts and underlines below.*

*The Joint Vision: "The levels of contaminants in the lake are dropping significantly. People are using the cleaner lake with confidence again— people are swimming and fishing, seniors are sitting on benches and talking, parents are tending babies and playing with older kids…* ~~No-body in the area is using toxic chemicals~~*—*<u>*Voluntary measures have drastically reduced the use of toxic chemicals at homes around the lake*</u>*. Everybody is taking responsibility for keeping the lake and the lakeshore clean. People from other parts of the city are coming by and talking about cleaning up pollution problems where they live."*

**8** **Build an agreement on the common ground you find.** Using the vision as a guide, it's time to start nailing down the details of an agreement that all sides are willing to implement. See the common ground you've found as the place where circles overlap ~

a little

more

Whether initially that common ground is a sliver or a big chunk, all sides to the conflict can stand on that ground and work together to expand it. When this process is really humming, people start to see themselves less as proponents of one side, than as allies working together on a common task. The conflict is no longer "Us Against Them" but "All of Us Against a Problem We Need to Solve."

As this happens, the process can create its own momentum. People become less defensive and more creative. Often they get so committed to solving the common problem that they start coming up with options that didn't seem possible or ideas that couldn't be seen before the process started. When suspicion and anger diminish, people become more willing to accept good ideas and insights no matter who suggests them.

*Dialogue*

In the negotiations with the land developer and the County Planning Director, we all got committed to the process of creating common ground. I came up with a part of the solution that the developer might have suggested— and he proposed a part that could have come from the environmentalists.

*creates the*

*opportunity*

*for solutions*

Expand common ground through dialogue, not debate. The goal of debate is to prove yourself right. The goal of dialogue is to create enough mutual understanding and trust that people can discover and enlarge areas of shared agreement. Dialogue creates the opportunity for solutions that last, because they're built, not on points scored, but on genuinely shared positions

*that last.*

and values. If you hit a road-block, go back to the shared vision, and, from there, try to find another way around the obstacle. Sometimes it's important to suggest face-saving outs that make it easier for people to climb down off earlier, strongly-held positions.

*At Lake McChubb, several homeowners complain that the nontoxic weedkillers don't kill all the weeds. The students and other homeowners remind them of the benefits to hundreds of people of a lake without weedkiller chemicals in it, and point out that everybody's lawns may now have a few weeds. A neighbor with a sense of humor presents each of the holdouts with a weeding trowel and set of silly instructions on how to pull a weed out of the ground. People laugh. The opposition fades.*

**9** **Commit to carrying out the agreement.** As new common ground appears, keep adding details and expanding it further. It's not necessary—or realistic—that the circles will ever overlap completely. When all sides agree there's enough common ground to resolve the conflict, they write up an agreement and commit to carrying it out—together.

Those nine steps aren't going to work perfectly every time. But I guarantee they'll raise your chances of success in dealing with any conflict. It's amazing to me that establishing trust and building agreements from there is sometimes called unrealistic. I've seen the process work far too often to believe that. To me, the people who are unrealistic are those who think the old dukes-up, winner-take-all approaches to conflict are going to work at all, despite all the evidence that they just keep the conflicts alive and coming back again and again.

Some people who won't try trust-building are frightened by the risks involved. They've got a point. It does take more courage to build trust than to square off and fight. Fighting is relatively easy; it's what everybody knows. The path I'm suggesting calls forth the very best that's in you, and can produce results better than you—or your "opponent"—could possibly get from fighting.

✔ When people get stuck in conflict, it's usually because they can't get past their emotional baggage to work things out.

✔ The best way to resolve conflicts is *not* to try to outwit or overpower people—winning by making somebody lose can create losers on all sides.

✔ Handle your "inside stuff." You're in charge of your reactions to other people, no matter what the provocation.

✔ Look for stereotypes and negative judgments you may have of people who oppose you. Hanging on to your judgments gives the other person no chance to improve.

✔ A conflict is like an iceberg—7/8 of it is invisible. The more aware you are of hidden issues—including your own—the better chance you'll have to resolve the visible conflict.

✔ Build trust. When people trust each other, they become less defensive, more honest—and much more able to solve a conflict.
> ~ *Building trust means being open.*
> ~ *Build trust through respect and caring.*

✔ Look for easy fixes.

✔ Confirm the issues that are still in conflict.
> ~ *Outline the differences accurately.*
> ~ *Explain the rationale for your positions completely. Be open about any uncertainties or downsides you see in them, and urge others to do the same.*
> ~ *Get more information if you need it.*

✔ Help people create a shared vision for a solution to the conflict that all sides can willingly accept.

✔ Build an agreement on the common ground you find.

✔ Commit to carrying out the agreement.

✔ Go for it. The strategy outlined above doesn't work every time, but it will improve your chances of success in resolving conflicts.

CHAPTER TEN

# Lead–Who, You?

Here's "leadership" way in the back of the book, but the secret is that the whole book is about leadership. Everything you've read so far is something leaders need to know, even though it's also valuable for team members or for people working alone. It's only this chapter and the next that deal with things that may be more important for leaders than everybody else.

**Who are "leaders"?** In school, people may think it's the class officers, the team captains, the most popular kids, or the straight-A scholars. When people think of leaders in the larger world, they think of people who've done something very big or dramatic. But leadership is much broader than this. It's not some rare quality, possessed only by a few. The place to look for leaders is not just in history books, on a television screen, and in newspapers. Look also across the street, in the room—and in the mirror.

Yes, some people are better leaders than others. But the Giraffe view is that just about everybody, if they choose, can learn the skills, and has the potential to lead when they are called to lead—even people who might not see themselves as leaders at all.

**What's "leadership"?** The dictionary says that leadership means "to guide, to have charge of." But at the Giraffe Project, and in this book, leadership is much more than giving direction and exercising authority; it has a focus of service. We say: *Leadership is motivating and guiding people to work toward the common good with more focus and power than they would otherwise have.*

Sarah Swagart's effort to build a skateboarding park is a good example of leadership. So is Lois Gibbs' fight against pollution at Love Canal and Craig Kielburger's campaign against child slavery. In fact, all the Giraffes you've read about are good leaders.

Learning to lead is not a process in which you start from scratch—like learning to speak a new language, or playing some game you've never seen before. Leadership skills build on who you already are—your personality, skills, abilities and experience. No two people lead in the same way, so there are many different ways to be a good leader.

You may not pick up all the steps quickly, like a new dance, but you can get better at it over time. The basic skills and techniques you need to know are in this book. Then it's practicing, watching good models, and improving as you go.

**But what if you don't *want* to be a leader?** Well, you certainly have a choice. It's clear that important things are done by individuals operating entirely on their own—inventors, artists and scientists come to mind. And if everyone wanted to lead all the time, nothing would get done; good team players are essential.

*If everyone wanted to lead all the time, nothing would get done.*

But even if you never expect to lead, the need for leadership can arise suddenly and there may be nobody but you to fill that need.

Maybe you'll be working on a project and, with time running out, you'll see everything start to fall apart because nobody's taking responsibility, or because the people in charge are leading in the wrong direction. Maybe you're with a group that's about to be led into doing something you know is really dumb or cruel, and nobody else is challenging that. Maybe you'll just be minding your own business and some crisis will land on your head.

At times like that, there's no point in wishing you were somebody or someplace else. You know something's got to be done and you can see nothing's going to happen unless you make a move. The story of Lois Gibbs and Love Canal in Chapter One is a good example of this kind of unexpected leadership. Here's another ~

When 15-year-old Roxanne Black was diagnosed with lupus—a serious, chronic disease—she was devastated. She wanted to talk to someone who really understood what she was going through, someone her own age who also had lupus. She decided to organize a support group for lupus patients.

She didn't find that personal friend she was looking for, at least

not right away, but she did find a whole new mission for her life—other people with serious illnesses were looking for someone who understood, just as she was. They felt alone, especially those suffering from little-understood illnesses.

Black formed the Friends' Health Connection, which she has built into a national support network for thousands of people with serious illnesses, injuries or disabilities. The Connection links them to someone with whom they can share information, while they keep each other's spirits up. She also organized a semiannual auction that has raised thousands of dollars for lupus research and public education.

While in college, Black suffered a kidney failure, not unusual among people with lupus. Not one to waste time, she did computer work for Friends' Health Connection while undergoing five-times-a-day kidney dialysis treatments.

An organ transplant was necessary if she was to survive; her sister donated the needed kidney. After the operation, Black launched a campaign to get the word out that organ donations are down and that thousands of critically ill people need more of their fellow citizens to sign organ donor cards.

Friends' Health Connection is now going into 27 hospitals where people can connect with supportive new friends right from their hospital rooms, immediately after being diagnosed.

The stories of Lois Gibbs and Roxanne Black show how people who never expected to lead can be thrown into action by events they never anticipated. Even if you're convinced you're not a leader, don't assume you'll never play that role—you can never know for sure what's going to come your way.

Sometimes people become leaders, not because they're blind-sided by a sudden event, but because they grow into the role; they'll be members of a group or team and they'll start motivating others and contributing to decisions, just because that comes naturally. They take on additional responsibility; people appreciate what they're doing and start asking them to do more. A lot of Giraffes start this way, like Louise Stanley did ~

B rooklyn's East New York section used to be a good place to live. In 1967 Louise Stanley became a proud homeowner there, working at the post office and raising her six children. But the area began to deteriorate and, after years of neglect, many buildings had been aban-

doned or even torched. Vacant lots had turned into trash heaps. Drug dealers were taking over the empty buildings. In a city where good affordable housing is practically a myth, Louise Stanley couldn't stand seeing buildings empty. Remembering when the neighborhood was friendly and open, she yearned to get rid of the criminals who had

moved in. So Stanley attended a meeting of ACORN, the Association of Community Organizations for Reform Now. She'd come intending to listen. She soon found herself raising her hand, speaking her mind and volunteering for assignments. Within weeks she was leading the first East New York ACORN group.

Within two years Stanley and her ACORN group had organized a community of people to reclaim and renovate abandoned buildings in the neighborhood. Families moved into empty city-owned buildings. Neighbors provided power and water. Volunteers like Stanley worked with the families on rehabbing the buildings.

City Hall had the new residents arrested. Stanley, by then a savvy activist, was pleased. She alerted the press and the resulting furor put the city on the defensive. Here were poor people fixing up abandoned apartments, and the city was arresting them?

Stanley negotiated with the city, and a deal was struck. ACORN agreed not to break into any more buildings. The city agreed to set up the Mutual Housing Authority of New York to give abandoned housing units to community groups for rehabilitation. The city also provided $2.7 million to buy renovation materials for 58 buildings. Not a bad result for a novice organizer. Louise Stanley says, "The bottom line is getting people to realize that success is possible." That's leadership.

Louise Stanley had no idea she'd end up leading a movement that would reclaim a good hunk of East New York from urban decay. For her, as for many Giraffes, leadership "happened." When she found herself in the middle of an issue she cared a lot about, she rolled up her sleeves and went to work, becoming a leader along the way.

Has leadership ever "happened" to you? If it has, what's the story?

• • • • • • • • • • • • • • • • • • • • • • • • • • • • • • • • • • • • • • • • • • • • •

**When is leadership needed?** There are plenty of times when a team or group can operate just fine without any formal leadership. Other times, strong direction may be needed. What's usually best is something in between.

It's a sliding scale: *Leadership should become more direct as the seriousness of the situation a group is in begins to go beyond its confidence to handle it.*

Consider that idea in a specific situation ~

You and some friends are going for a hike. It's a clear summer day, all of you are strong hikers. The decisions that must be made on the trip (when to stop for lunch, for example) are so small that there's no need for anyone to be the "leader."

But now let's say that four hours into the hike a sudden lightning storm comes barreling over a nearby ridge. Rain falls in sheets and on the way back down the trail you find that a bridge has been washed away. You can't find another way across the stream, and it's getting late. As the situation gets more serious, and the hour gets later, the informal "no leader" system might not work as well as it did on the way up. It might be time for one or several of the group members to step forward and lead. These leaders may or may not be the most technically competent in outdoor skills—reading the map, for example, should be left to the person best at doing that, whether she's the leader or not. What the leader needs to do is stay calm, keep others calm, and guide the group to make the decisions and take the actions it needs to take.

Now let's say that Kendra slips in the mud and sprains her ankle. David, now soaked to the skin and scared, starts mumbling and acting strange. As the situation worsens, and as the confidence of the group to handle it decreases, the group's leadership needs to be even more direct; there's no time to debate every decision in the fading light and, even if there were, the calming and guiding function of good leadership is now essential.

The bottom line is: what group members need to watch is not just the seriousness of the situation they're in, and not just the confidence they feel in coping— but the balance between the two. If every person on that hike is experienced in dealing with crises and making decisions under stress, then informal, low-key leadership— or none at all—might continue to work no matter how serious things get. It's when the group's confidence is not up to handling a situation that the need for more direct leadership arises. And the more overwhelmed the group is, the more direct the leadership should be.

Here's how that might play out on the Lake McChubb project ~

*Assuming that organizing a work plan for this project goes smoothly, there's probably little need for leadership; the decisions that need to be made can all be made in group meetings. But say the City Council asks the group to present its project for approval at a formal meeting. The local television station says they'll send a camera crew. This is a pretty big deal for most of the group, and many extra details must be handled. While an experienced group might handle all this fine without formal leadership, a less seasoned group might well want to put one or two of its members in charge, at least of preparing for the Council meeting.*

Have you ever been part of a group when conditions suddenly worsened, prompting a need for someone to take more charge? If you have, what happened?

**Leadership style.** Your individual personality gives your leadership a distinctive style. There are as many different styles of leadership as there are leaders. Rose, for example, is a woman of few words; she lets her example do the talking. Dylan, on the other hand, tends to explain everything three times; Amanda's always cracking jokes when she's leading a meeting; Emily's always serious. These personality differences are reflected in how each of them leads.

It's important to understand your leadership style—so you can make use of its advantages, and turn possible disadvantages into strengths. Let's say, for example, that you've always had an interest in details. Every pencil you own is sharp. Your socks are perfectly matched and folded. You're never late for an appointment. Your leadership style is equally thorough and precise. There are plusses and minuses to this, and you need to be aware of both. No one in any group you lead ever has to be concerned that you'll forget the hot dog buns or give directions that get people lost. But you need to remember that your insistence on quadruple checking can drive people nuts. You need to know where to draw the line between being competent and being a pain in the neck.

Here's a Giraffe with a distinctive style ~

Hazel Wolf was born in 1898 and has been leading actions for social justice and environmental conservation all her life. Wolf is a little old lady with an impish sense of humor. Her voice is so small she almost needs a microphone in a living room. Yet she can hold a thousand people on the edge of their seats. Because she's relentless, really listens and truly cares, she inspires fierce loyalty, and can bend policy makers to her will. Wolf knows exactly how to use her power as a little-old-lady-with-a-huge-heart and a mischievous twinkle in her eye.

Don't try to change your personality to fit someone else's image of what a "leader" should be. If you try to act like an old pro when you're not, for example, you'll probably lose support instead of gaining it. Your leadership style must be genuine. If the people following you know that what they see is what they get, it will help them trust you as a leader. If you're faking it, the people you're trying to lead will sense that and it'll be much harder for them to trust you and cooperate with you.

Here's a Giraffe who led as herself—a worried kid ~

When Melissa Poe was nine, she saw a TV program that showed how polluted the world might become if we continue on the course we're on. That worried her, so she wrote the President of the United States, asking him to help stop pollution. She got

a form letter back—and it was on another subject. Melissa wasn't about to be ignored just because she was a kid. So she called an outdoor sign company and asked them to put her letter to the President on a billboard. The company was so impressed they put her letter up on dozens of billboards and convinced other sign companies to do the same in other cities. Melissa went on to lead a club called Kids for a Clean Environment that grew to over 300,000 members.

Melissa Poe may have gotten the brush-off the first time around, but it was writing and calling as a *kid* that turned out to be the key to her effectiveness. Her voice got through because it was *not* that of a polished politician or lobbyist, and other kids followed her lead.

**What's *your* leadership style?** Your intuition can help you identify your leadership style. I use an exercise to help people find their styles. It relies on metaphors, using the word for one thing to describe another, to suggest a likeness between them—like calling someone a "pig" for bad table manners or a "chicken" for running away from danger.

Sit down with a friend and imagine yourself in any leadership role you've played. Then your friend asks you, "When you're leading—if you were an animal, what animal would you be?" Answer with the first image that pops into your mind. You might say: "I'm a sheepdog," or "I'm a chimp." Think about what you've said and see if you can find reasons for the match your intuition just made. You might say, "When I lead I'm a sheepdog because I'm always circling around, keeping everything and everyone going" or "I'm a chimp because I keep things light and funny." Your friend repeats the same question using other metaphors, such as cars, food, and musical instruments. The answers can be very informative: "I'm a Volvo because I'm really solid." "I'm a combo pizza because I use all kinds of styles, depending on the situation." "I'm a trumpet, because I make a lot of noise and I'm really clear about what I have to say."

Does your friend agree with your assessments? Do you see your style as "mule," but your friend thinks "eagle?" Do you see "electric guitar," but your friend says "violin?" Talk about those differences and about your choices. Consider your reasons for those choices and think about your friend's reactions. Did the two of you agree most of the time? If not, who's seeing the true you? Use what you learn to refine your style.

Oh, go ahead. Try it. Nobody but your friend is looking.

**Why lead?** Leadership can take your time and effort away from things you might rather do. Being that visible can bring you unwanted attention and criticism. You could be blamed for failures. You could lose friends. There are a lot of reasons for keeping your head down and letting somebody else take the flak. So why would you ever do it?

I can tell you why *I* do it. Leading is my best chance to help shape tomorrows that I want to live in, that I want my kids—and their kids and *theirs*—to live in. There are things that I'd like to see happen, that won't happen if I just *wish* they would. Of-

*Leading is your best chance to shape tomorrows you want.*

ten those "things" are local—a problem I can take on that helps my community. I've had other opportunities to lead on issues that are national, or even international. Whether the opportunity is small or large, using the leadership skills and experience I have often does makes a difference, whether I've seen that immediately or not. Even when an effort I've led has failed, knowing I've stepped up and contributed all I can is important to me.

Leading also gives you hands-on experience at making decisions, managing plans, motivating team members and resolving conflicts. Having these skills, knowing that you have them, and seeing them work in the real world, can greatly enhance your self-confidence.

But it's not just building and using these skills that brings that confidence. It's also the experience of accepting the lead role and seeing that you've made a difference.

When you lead there may be times when you have to say "No" or make other decisions that will disappoint or anger other people. There could be times when you have to stand up and speak when you really want to hide under a rock. There might be times when the people you need to come through for you don't, and times when you have to stay on task when you'd love to take a break. Every time you come through such situations, you'll be stronger and you'll build your faith in your own competence. And that self-confidence doesn't disappear when the immediate challenge or project is over. It's there every day of your life, and in every part of your life.

Here's a guy who's taken enormous risks to lead ~

To the guys he used to hang with on Baltimore streets, Charles Spann is a fool. He used to be a "big man"—on his block—doing deals, making fists full of money. Spann's early "success" earned him a ticket to a correction center, where he spent two years thinking only of getting back to the streets. But one staff member there saw strength and spirit in Spann and got the teenager into a rehab program called Fresh Start. There, Spann did a turnaround that's brought him a lot of flak from lifelong friends.

In his new life as President of Tico Enterprises, Spann now deals with bankers, retailers and media. He's lining up investments, making sales and doing publicity for the company's "environmentally and socially benevolent" wood products and its work restoring boats and building docks. He's had to learn business, communications, and management skills—none of it's been easy for a guy who hated school.

The alternative, he points out, isn't so easy either—dying on cement, with a chalk line around your body. "I hate to hear about young black guys getting killed," he told a reporter. "They just say before the end of the news 'It was suspected to be drug-related.'"

Charles Spann will tell you that all the challenges of his new life are worth it, and that the best part is showing kids who are still doing deals on the street corners that there's another way.

Have you ever done something you knew was right even though your friends didn't want you to do it? What happened? How did that feel?

◆••••••••••••••••••••••••••••••••••••••••••••••••••••◆

**Team play.** Being a good member of a team led by others is a big part of getting any project done well. When you're on a team, you can contribute to good morale, maintain a positive attitude, keep your commitments, and pitch in to help with the tougher tasks.

Give the team leader at least the benefit of the doubt when the first difficult decisions must be made. If you've got a complaint about how things are going, don't go along with one eye cocked for a place to bail out, or grumbling under your breath or out loud; bring up your concern and discuss it openly. In some situations, the leader might very well be in above his head, and it then becomes the responsibility of the whole group to discuss that situation and either help the leader do better, or choose a new leader.

If you're used to leading, but for this project or event you're not in charge, give your leader the respect she needs to do her job. That's especially important if it's someone with less experience at leading than you have. It's tough for a new leader to deal with a more experienced person who is judging or condescending. Model the kind of support you like to have when you're leading. Good leaders can shift easily into and out of leadership roles, depending on what's needed at the time.

✔ Good leaders help people to act with more focus and power than they would otherwise have.

✔ Just about everybody can lead when they're called to.

✔ Leadership skills build on who you already are.

✔ Leadership is something you get better at over time.

✔ Even if you don't *expect* to lead, the need to do so can arise unexpectedly.

✔ Sometimes people become leaders by growing into the role.

✔ Leadership should become more direct as the seriousness of the situation a group is in begins to go beyond its confidence to handle it.

✔ Understand your leadership style, use its advantages, and turn any disadvantages into strengths.

✔ Your leadership style must be genuine.

✔ The benefits of leadership ~

~ It's a special chance to make a difference.
~ It's an opportunity to learn useful skills.
~ The self-confidence that comes with leading is a valuable lifelong asset.

✔ When you're a team member, contribute to team morale, keep your commitments, and pitch in to help with the tough tasks. Give the team leader at least the initial benefit of the doubt when difficult decisions must be made. And if you've got a complaint about the leader, make it to her directly.

CHAPTER ELEVEN

# What It Takes to Lead Well

No one expects you to already have all the leadership skills and qualities described in this chapter. Becoming a good leader is about learning and growing—watching role models, gaining experience and building on what you've got. The learning never stops.

Here's a look at two people who lead very well indeed ~

Dennis Littky had been the much-praised principal of a model school on Long Island, but he was burned out. He decided to just learn to live in the woods, so he moved to an unplumbed mountain cabin in Winchester, New Hampshire.

The town of Winchester had a high unemployment rate; many, many residents were on welfare. Its high school, Thayer, reflected the town's troubles with a sky-high dropout rate. Thayer High was as down as the town—everything was broken, dirty or covered with graffiti. Students drank and smoked pot in the halls. It was a mess, but that wasn't Littky's problem; he was minding his own business, living the simple life out in the woods.

But it didn't take long for Littky to get restless. He started a newspaper. He became a state legislator. Then he got on the school board. When Thayer's principal resigned, Littky was ready to return to running a school.

Despite many townspeople's strong distrust of innovation, Littky was sure only radical change could save Thayer. In his first year, he did away with study halls, formed a Principal's advisory team of seniors and met personally with every student to design his/her curriculum, often bending the rules to create individual study plans that got kids revved to learn. Littky got his students apprenticeships with local businesses. He hired a carpenter to teach building skills to kids who were itching to do something "big and important with their hands." He was on his feet and everywhere at once, talking with kids one-on-one as a firm, guiding friend. His enthusiasm and commitment were contagious.

Morale and grades improved dramatically. And everybody in town was grateful, right? Wrong. Littky was fired by the conservative school board, who disapproved of his unorthodox ways. But instead of giving in, Littky rallied his supporters. That school board was voted out and replaced by pro-Littky members.

At Littky's Thayer, the percentage of seniors going on to college shot up 600%. Littky's reforms are now so successful that Thayer teachers travel the US, giving workshops on how to turn a school around.

Dennis Littky moved a whole town to act for the good of its kids. The political effort he led to replace the school board was only a small part of it. His real leadership success was with the kids. He threw out old ways of doing things at Thayer, put the kids first, and helped them recharge their confidence in themselves.

Dolly Kiffin says that she was "just a housewife back then," a Jamaica-born dressmaker raising six children at Broadwater Farm, a huge housing project outside London. The project was dirty, decaying, and dangerous. The young, who were mostly without jobs, terrified the old, who hid in their apartments. Tensions between black and white tenants, already high, intensified after the head of the ten-ants' association appeared on television spouting white-supremacist prejudices.

Kiffin wanted to end the hatred she saw in Broadwater Farm; she thought a sense of community would return to the 3,000 residents of the project if they tackled their problems together. They could start by helping the unemployed young people.

The Broadwater Farm Youth Association (BFYA) was formed after Kiffin led a series of meetings in her apartment. The first priority of the BFYA was creating a youth center. With a small grant from a local government agency, the Broadwater kids renovated an old fish and chips shop under the guidance of a local contractor, learning valuable building skills in the process.

From the beginning, Kiffin insisted that the BFYA center had to be something that would help bring the whole community together. When the kids wanted money for a pool table and arcade games, for example, Kiffin made a deal with them. They could have the equipment, but half the profits from the games had to be used to provide meals for senior citizens in the project. The BFYA not only took on the meals program but also provided free drivers for day trips the kids organized for the elderly. Young and old, blacks and whites, began to know one another.

Kiffin wasn't done yet. She said that government programs had been training young people for jobs that didn't exist. She suggested that the BFYA create jobs by training people to work for themselves. The young people in BFYA started small cooperative businesses that they owned and ran. As these businesses grew, they hired and trained new people. Over 100 young people were soon employed in seven co-op businesses that provided vital community services, and more co-ops were starting. Kiffin got a community garden going and pressured the local government into requiring that people from Broadwater Farm be hired to maintain it.

To the embarrassment of social-welfare experts and government bureaucrats, Dolly Kiffin's work has been extremely successful. She proved that low-income people could help themselves with only a minimum of government support. "We hadn't any qualifications at all," she said, "just our love for people. We put our whole selves into it."

For most of this time Kiffin has worked without pay. She now receives a salary, which she returns to the BFYA general fund. "I do it out of love for people," she says in her strong Jamaican accent, "regardless of what race they are—black or white or whatever. I did it out of determination, for I could not sit down and accept racism. I do it to show that ordinary grassroots people can do something to stop racism."

Leaders are real people, not super-beings. Kiffin is overly modest when she says, "We hadn't any qualifications at all," but she's making the point that she and her team just used what they had and what they knew. She grew into leadership, as we all can when the need arises, building on our own personalities, abilities and life experiences.

Littky and Kiffin are different people living in different circumstances in different parts of the world, but both have risen to the challenge to lead, and both have done it well.

What skills and personal qualities do Littky and Kiffin have that helped them lead their communities so well?

◆·······································································◆

## What Do Good Leaders Do?

Good leaders have a vision and can communicate it to others, enlisting their support in making the vision real. They can organize and plan a project, make good decisions and deal well with conflicts. They're courageous, caring, and responsible. These are skills and qualities already covered in this book; they're important for anyone, leader or not.

But there's more. Here's a list of other skills and qualities important to good leaders, compiled from watching a lot of leaders, and from my own experience. But no good leader *starts* with all these skills. They learn. They watch good models. They practice. They get better by trial and error. It all takes time. Don't think you need to be an expert in all of this now.

**1** **Good leaders inspire people to believe in themselves.** They motivate people to be at their best. They do that by seeing and encouraging people's strengths, and by believing in *everyone's* potential to succeed.

Calvin Bryant grew up on a farm, one of 16 kids of a Georgia sharecropper. He dropped out of school in the 8th grade and went to work, eventually building up a prosperous furniture repair business in Sarasota, Florida. He's a success. His community recognized that, naming him Small Businessman of the Year. That same year a teenager stole a lawnmower from Bryant's house. The thief was caught, and when Bryant went to court to identify him he told the judge, "Give him to me. I'll work with him." The judge thought he was nuts, but remanded the young man to Bryant's custody.

Bryant never doubted that the teen could turn his life around—that belief rubbed off on the ex-thief. Soon he was a valuable—and honest—employee in Bryant's company.

Bryant began going into prisons as a counselor and bringing prisoners out, giving them good jobs, counseling them, teaching them by his example that even a tough start in life won't stop a person determined to make it.

"They were making bad choices because they didn't know how to work with the system," Bryant says. "They didn't know what it had to offer, how to get what they needed legally." A basic part of that lack of knowledge was that most of them couldn't read and write. Bryant realized he could just work with lawbreakers forever, or he could also go straight for the next generation of potential prisoners—poor kids who weren't learning to read.

Bryant hired a teacher to run an after-school tutoring program for some of Sarasota's poorest kids. "I found out all kids at a very early age are very, very positive. They don't know about the 'can't dos.'" Bryant gives them positive reinforcement, good role models and a glimpse of life outside their own neighborhoods. He also gives them something to eat—he never knows if they get enough at home. "These kids," Bryant says firmly, "will not be dropouts."

Calvin Bryant increases both the confidence and the competence of the kids and ex-cons he works with—by believing in their potential, by acknowledging their abilities, and by giving them a powerful vision of what their lives could be like.

Has someone's faith in you ever helped you succeed? Has your faith in other people helped *them*? In each case, what happened?

**2** **Good leaders build trusting relationships with the people they lead.** Trust is the real basis of a good leader's authority. Leaders may have official positions and titles, but if those are the *only* sources of their authority, they're not going to evoke much enthusiasm from people. It's unlikely that Dolly Kiffin, Dennis Littky or Calvin Bryant would have succeeded if they hadn't gained the trust of the people they worked with. Especially if difficult decisions must be made and carried out, leadership based on titles and positions is far less effective than leadership based on trust. Trust between a leader and team members improves communications, calms fears, strengthens cooperation and moves people to do their best.

Have you ever been part of a group whose leader had authority over you—but whose motives and/or competence you didn't trust? How did you feel about following his lead? Did you work well with him? Have you been part of a group whose leader—with or without an official title—earned your trust? Were your responses to that leader different? If so, how?

It's easier to trust a leader who is *competent*. If I'm convinced the leader knows what she's doing, I'm much more likely to trust her to do the right thing in a crunch.

Trust is also built on *reliability*—knowing that people will do what they say they'll do. Leaders and team members all need to know they can count on each other. A leader who goes back on her word damages the trust team members have in her.

But for leaders (as for everybody), the real key to earning trust is *caring*. When people know a leader cares about them, they trust that she will keep their interests in mind. They become more likely to follow her lead, readier to give their best effort, and more willing to accept decisions they might not like.

Have you ever been in a group whose leader didn't seem to care about you personally? Have you been in a group whose leader obviously cared about you? Which one did you trust more? Which one were you more ready to follow?

Caring grows like yeast in bread. As a leader models putting himself into others' shoes, they pick up on his example and trust grows in the group as a whole. Without being pushy or intrusive, a good leader creates informal opportunities for group members to develop connections with each another—even if it's just stopping work to share stories. The more group members care about and trust each other, the better they work together.

**3** **Good leaders help people grow.** Good leaders recognize and encourage each person's strengths and find ways to engage those strengths in achieving the team's vision. A good leader, for example, would realize that Ann writes well and Karyn is good at graphics, and would encourage them to be the ones to create a brochure for the team's project.

If there are people who *aren't* skilled in their groups, good leaders find ways those team members can gain knowledge and experience.

Good leaders delegate jobs and authority, building people's skills and confidence. When group members know they're responsible for important parts of the action, they usually return the confidence that the leader's placed in them with increased enthusiasm and participation.

Think of a time when you've been trusted to carry out a vital part of a plan, and another when you've been allowed only to do stuff that doesn't matter. Has your role affected your commitment? If so, how?

◆••••••••••••••••••••••••••••••••••••••••••••••••••••◆

4 **Good leaders help build and maintain an atmosphere that's upbeat and respectful.** Everybody on a team has a responsibility to help create a positive atmosphere, but the leader needs to realize that she will probably have more influence on the group's spirit than anyone else. Good leaders know how to handle themselves in a crisis or a setback. They may feel discouraged, angry or upset, but they have a special responsibility to pull up their socks and model a positive, forward-looking response to trouble.

Say the newspaper has called your club "incompetent" and everybody's furious. Adding to that anger won't help—you need to get your team cooled down so you can all create a plan for reversing the bad PR.

5 **Good leaders don't abuse their authority.** Good leaders don't have to stand on their authority to put down a challenge—"I'm

the leader, so do what I told you!" Barring some crisis in which there's no time to get everybody's opinion on what to do, a good leader doesn't go off on solos; he takes in new information constantly from the team and is willing to change course if need be.

Needless to say—there's *never* any excuse for being rude just because you're the leader—that's a sure way to lose people's trust.

**6** **Good leaders are good managers.** What do good managers do? Here's a quick checklist ~

~ They help their groups stay focused. If a group gets distracted by side issues, or bogged down in petty disputes, it's the leader's job to get everyone back on course.

~ They keep on top of plans and schedules. Responsibilities can be shared, but the buck still stops with the leader. It's her job to make sure that group members have done the research, double-checked the plans, bought the supplies, arranged for the transportation, etc.

~ They anticipate potential problems—such as missing volunteers and supplies—and have fall-back options ready.

~ They make sure that information is accurate, complete and delivered on time to the people who need to know it. They double check to make sure that complex messages are understood.

~ They stay tuned to how team members are doing, so they can give people direction or support when they need it, and they can spot and try to head off potential conflicts before they get out of hand.

**7** **Good leaders use their hearts as well as their heads.** Using both is important for anyone, but it's especially so for a good leader. Trying to lead—or to live—by using only your intellect is like trying to play a song using only a drum. Good leaders are intuitive as well as logical. They're enthusiastic and visionary—and they're well organized and attentive to details. They can both show their feelings and control their emotions, when that's what is needed. They're attuned to the feelings of others. They're good at finding common ground with people they disagree with—and they can put together a well-reasoned case in an argument.

Using your heart and your head means stretching your imagination and your spirit, balancing hard-edged thinking with flying by the seat of your pants. It means taking responsibility, not just for reaching goals, but for your impact on people's lives.

Using both the head and the heart means running an efficient, productive meeting—and asking for David's opinion when you realize he's too shy to speak up. As a project moves along, it's sensing that Deborah is burning out, but won't say so—and finding someone who can give her a hand. It's pointing out to Tim a mistake he's made—and telling him about the last time you blew it too.

Here are two leaders who use both heads and hearts ~

S tarting with $100 and two horses, Eileen Szychowski (pronounced sha-HUS-ky) built Camelot, a unique horsemanship program in Scottsdale, Arizona for people with physical disabilities. People of all ages come there to learn riding; some are in wheelchairs; some are

blind; all are riding horses for the first time.

Many of the people Szychowski asked to support Camelot thought horseback riding was too risky for people with disabilities. Disabled herself, Szychowski disagrees. She told her critics that you have to risk to grow, and that, for someone who can't walk, riding a horse helps them feel stronger and in control.

A childhood bout with a neurological disease left Szychowski unable to get around without crutches or a wheelchair. At 21 she met a disabled horseman who inspired her to return to her original goal of working with horses.

She trained as a riding and outdoor education instructor. When she was turned down for a mule trip through the Grand Canyon because she was disabled, Szychowski challenged the decision and went on to become the first disabled mounted Park Ranger in Grand Canyon Park. To do so, she had to pass the same tests as all the other rangers.

Given her determination, it's no surprise that Szychowski's risky venture into teaching is succeeding too. Because the classes at Camelot are free, she expects all students to "give something back" by doing community service work. Many choose to work on Camelot's Visiting Critters Project, which tours schools, hospitals and nursing homes with an array of exotic pets.

Szychowski and the other instructors with disabilities are wonderful models for Camelot's students. It's all part of her desire to show that a disability doesn't have to stop you. "You don't know how wonderful it is to feel ordinary," she said. "You see a child so terribly frail. As soon as she can control a thousand-pound animal, she starts to change."

John Croyle was a top defensive end for the University of Alabama's legendary coach, Bear Bryant. After Croyle's last game his teammates say, "See you in the pros." Croyle is that good. Does he (a) sign on as a pro football player for megabucks, or (b) go into debt to start a ranch for abused and abandoned kids?

Giraffe John Croyle is the guy who picked (b). He started Big Oak Boys' Ranch with a wish, a prayer and some miraculously timely financial angels. Two days before

Croyle had to come up with $45,000 to buy the ranch, a dentist from Birmingham arrived with $15,000 in hand. Then, with time really running out on the clock, a former 'Bama teammate donated his $30,000 signing bonus from the New England Patriots.

Croyle started small, with five boys in the ranch's old four-room house. He had no experience with social workers, health inspectors or the juvenile justice system. When an official from the welfare department dropped in unexpectedly and asked to see his license, the obliging Croyle pulled out his driver's license. He didn't know he had to have a state license for housing kids.

The ranch grew to six large brick homes, each with houseparents caring for eight boys of various ages. It's a working ranch where the boys raise much of their food. Croyle's 6'7" frame is everywhere, helping with farm work and homework, playing a fast game of basketball. He says, "They've never had anybody who trusted or depended on them. Now they do, and once somebody believes in you, half the battle is over."

Since 1975 over a thousand boys have lived at the ranch, some for days and some for years. He finds boys in jails, hospitals, abusive homes and once, in a railroad boxcar. And he's started a similar ranch for girls.

Croyle promises new arrivals that he'll stick with them until they're grown. And if each new kid tries to be the best person he or she can be, they've got Croyle for life. When they graduate from school, Croyle helps them find jobs, get college scholarships or enlist in the services. He knows where most of his graduates are and what they're doing.

A local judge said, "If everybody had as much interest in their own children as John Croyle does in *any* kid, we wouldn't have delinquency in this country. It's that simple."

Szychowski and Croyle are both caring and tough, emotional and logical. They're both good at communicating a vision and at managing complex projects.

Do you tend to rely more on your head or your heart? Where do you think the leaders at your school or in your community would fall on a scale that ran from "all head" at one end to "all heart" at the other?

✔ Becoming a good leader is about watching role models and gaining experience. The learning never stops.

✔ Anyone can become a leader at the level they might need to lead, building on their own personality and life experience.

✔ Good leaders have vision and know how to communicate it to enlist others. They can organize and plan a project, make good decisions and deal well with conflicts.

✔ Good leaders inspire people to believe in themselves, motivating them to be at their best.

✔ Leadership based on titles and positions is far less effective than leadership based on trust. Good leaders build trusting relationships with the people they lead by being competent, reliable and caring.

✔ Good leaders help people grow by recognizing, encouraging and engaging each person's strengths, and by delegating jobs and authority.

✔ Good leaders help build and maintain an atmosphere that's upbeat and respectful—and they don't abuse their authority.

✔ Good leaders are good managers ~
~ keeping their groups focused,
~ staying on top of plans and schedules,
~ anticipating potential problems,

~ making sure that information is accurate, complete and delivered on time to the people who need to know it,
~ double-checking to make sure that complex messages are
understood,
~ staying tuned to how team members are doing.

✔ Good leaders use what's in their hearts as well as what's in
their heads. Trying to lead—or to live—by using only your intellect
is like trying to play a song using only a drum.

**Here are some words on leadership
from the Giraffe Project's treasury of quotes ~**

*Charismatic leaders make us think, 'Oh, if only I could do that, be like that.' True leaders make us think, 'If they can do that, then... I can too.' They do not make people into followers, but into new leaders.*
—John Holt

*You can't make people do anything. You've got to help them want to.*
—Giraffe Edie Lewis

*Leadership is the ... quality which enables people ... to stand up and pull the rest of us over the horizon.*
—James L. Fisher

*You can't give people pride, but you can provide the kind of understanding that makes people look to their inner strengths and find their own sense of pride.*
—Giraffe Charleszetta Waddles

*Greatness is not standing above our fellows and ordering them around—it is standing with them and helping them to be all they can be.*
—G. Arthur Keough

**A chilling look at bad political leadership ~**
*Why should some poor slob on a farm want to risk his life in a war when the best he can get out of it is to come back to his farm in one piece? ... It is the leaders of a country who determine the policy, and it is always a simple matter to drag the people along, whether it is a democracy or a fascist dictatorship or a parliament or a communist dictatorship. Voice or no voice, the people can always be brought to the bidding of the leaders. That is easy. All you have to do is tell them that they are being at-tacked, and denounce the pacifists for lack of patriotism and exposing the country to danger. It works the same in any country.*
—Hermann Goering at the Nuremberg trials

**~ and a thought-provoking idea about international leadership:**
*I wonder, if we in the United States were to concentrate—as our over-whelming major priority—on making ourselves the best possible society we can be, whether the nations of the world might once again, without any pressure except the influence of example, begin to emulate us. But that would require us to be willing, at some risk, to recapture the ideal-ism that once made this nation so great.*
—M. Scott Peck M.D

CHAPTER TWELVE

# Where Do You Go From Here?

**W**hen you complete your project, before you move on, stop and celebrate. It's time to acknowledge what you've done— time for a party. Too often, we race ahead, forgetting to stop and enjoy what we've accomplished. A lot of us are really bad at patting ourselves on the back, no matter how much we might deserve a good pat. Anyone who knows me would tell you I'm good at forgetting this one. But it's important to everyone's well-being, including my own, so I do stop and celebrate—when I'm reminded to. So I'm reminding *you*—kick back now and congratulate your team and yourself on what you've achieved.

Whatever form your celebration takes, invite other students and faculty, invite friends, relatives, community members—and don't forget the people you met during the project. During the celebration, look back at the high spots and the low ones—celebrate that you made it through them all. Put out photos, clippings or other reminders of the project. If you have video about it, run the tape. Have a great time—just don't forget that this party's about celebrating your achievement.

*The McChubb team, not surprisingly, has their celebration at the lake. They invite all the neighbors, the 6th graders, the retirees—everybody who's been involved in the project. The mayor shows up for another run with the mower. The reporter who wrote a story in the paper and the* *camera crew that filmed the project's kick-off join the line for a piece of a big cake that's shaped like McChubb. Every team member is wearing a "Keep Lake McChubb Clean" tee shirt as they swap stories—and watch people swimming and fishing, seniors sitting on the benches and talking, and parents tending babies and playing with older kids. A family from the other side of town stops by and asks for advice on cleaning up the stream that goes through <u>their</u> neighborhood.*

As part of your celebration, talk about how your project went. How close to your vision did you come? Were there obstacles or resources that surprised you along the way? What did you learn about your community? About the people you worked with? About yourself? What, if anything, would you do differently if you could?

◆ ● ● ● ● ● ● ● ● ● ● ● ● ● ● ● ● ● ● ● ● ● ● ● ● ● ● ● ● ● ● ● ● ● ● ● ● ● ● ● ● ● ● ● ● ● ● ● ● ● ● ● ● ● ● ● ● ● ◆

**W**elcome to the Community of Caring. Doing your own service project is a big step into an important world. In taking that step—in carrying out a personal commitment to the common good—you've joined a special community of people. It's not a community of place, like a neighborhood. It's a community of spirit, of people who care and who act on their caring. This community has just grown—you're now a member and so are your teammates.

The other members are thousands of people like those you've met in this book. Having joined them in courageous, caring service, your own life may be changed forever. You know now that you can do more than be concerned, you can cause change. It's like riding a bicycle—once you know how, you know how. You look at any bike, and you know you can ride it. Now you can look at other things that concern you and know you can affect them. I hope it's now impossible for you to ever just hunker down and complain instead of sticking your neck out to take courageous, caring action.

**W**hat's next? You know that leading a meaningful life isn't a spectator sport, so a good answer to this question is more questions: What needs to be done? What else are you concerned about?

The world is full of needs, and they're all opportunities to serve. Think of all the other issues that came up in the brainstorming you did in Chapter Two. How about taking on one of those concerns now? It could be something you discovered in the course of doing your project or something you've been thinking about for a long time.

If your next project matches the first one in scale and complexity, you know what to do. But if the next one—or the project after it, or the one after *that*—is of a much larger scale and complexity, there are some things to consider ~

~ Make *very* sure you care enough about the issue to sustain your commitment. Bigger projects are bigger commitments.

~ Get help. You may have done a small project on your own or with a small team, but a major one usually takes more people. Attract them by communicating the strength of your commitment and a clear, concrete vision.

~ Build connections with people tackling the issue in other places. Use the Internet to find related Websites and to make email connections. What works for somebody else working on a similar project may work for you, and vice-versa. And you may want to join forces—it's true that there's strength in unity.

~ If the project could take a really long time, break it down into stages. Look at what needs to change first and start there, scheduling the rest of the project for later stages.

~ No matter how much there is to be done and how eager people are to get started, take time to create a vision of the results you want.

~ No matter how big the project is and how many people are involved, take the time to build trusting relationships with them.

~ Planning for bigger projects can get extremely complex. There are more possibilities to think about, more people to deal with, more goals and steps in the action. Use the vision as your guide for keeping all the action on course.

*Do something silly to get everybody laughing again.*

~ As projects get bigger, some people get formal and starchy. They start debating instead of dialoguing. If you find yourself or anybody on your team freezing up, take a deep breath, loosen up and do something silly to get yourself and everybody else laughing again. Don't let the size of the project cause people to forget to have fun.

~ The bigger the project, the more "icebergs" there can be—buried issues are everywhere, and it's important to be aware of them.

~ Because conflict is almost inevitable in larger projects—and also more complex and difficult—it's important that you and your team are trained and ready to deal with it. It's a good idea to role-play foreseeable conflicts. Use the guidance in Chapter Nine to do this.

~ *Leading* large projects requires the same basic skills and qualities as leading small ones, but management is more daunting. Leaders of large projects are managing and tracking more people, more dates, more details and need to stay on top of all of it.

**L**obbying. In larger projects, you may need to deal with government agencies and elected officials, convincing them that your project is worth their support. Advocating a cause to government officials is called "lobbying." You can lobby with letters, faxes, email and telephone calls, but making personal visits to decision-makers will be the most effective way to interest them. A courteous, well-planned presentation by a concerned young activist can astonish and intrigue them—consider your age a plus.

The moves you make as a lobbyist are just common sense ~

- ~ Find out who the decision-makers are for your issue—- they're the ones you want to connect with.

- ~ Check out the dates when key decisions that affect your project will be made—there's no point in lobbying the day *after* the decision.

- ~ Present good reasons for your point of view. If government money would be involved, show the costs of what you propose. If you're lobbying in person, do a "leave behind" that sums up your points, and perhaps a page or two of key statistics, recommendations, maps or news clips.

- ~ Never underestimate the power of letters, faxes, email or phone calls to officials. At a minimum, they're counted and summarized. But avoid mass-produced messages if you can—- personal ones are more impressive.

- ~ Elected officials read the *Letters to the Editor* page in the local papers, so send your opinions to the papers too. Check their deadlines and length limits so you have a better chance of getting printed.

- ~ One-on-one or small-group lobbying sessions are less formal than a speech, but most of the information in Chapter Eight on giving a speech applies. For example, dress conservatively so the official doesn't use your appearance as an excuse not to listen to you.

- ~ Be confident. I've worked on a Senator's staff and watched citizen-lobbyists get more notice in officials' offices than professional lobbyists, whose faces and views are all too well known. Public officials want to know what real people think about issues, and young people who are new voters, or close to voting age, are the future of the electorate—your opinion counts.

*The moves you make as a lobbyist are just common sense.*

# What If You Mess Up?

**You can do everything this book suggests
to make your projects successful,
but you can never reduce the risks to zero.
You can still "fail."**

A lot of people let even small failures stop them, but the people who get the most done in the world view a failure as a temporary setback. That viewpoint keeps them moving forward rather than knocking them out. They *use* failures as valuable guidance for course corrections. They figure out what went wrong and why, make the changes they need to make, and they keep on keeping on.

Operational setbacks—missing a deadline, raising less money than you need, being turned down by someone whose help is important—are part of most ventures. If there are no failures at all, it could mean that you aren't taking enough chances, aren't pushing beyond your old competency levels. To quote Coleman Hawkins, "If you don't make mistakes you aren't really trying." He may have been talking to fellow musicians, but the message applies to all of us. Don't let yourself or your team be KO'd when things go wrong.

**Get up and go on.**

## What's the point?

If and when your group suffers a setback,
use it to learn something, not as a reason for quitting.
Go back to the vision and use its power
to renew enthusiasm—then adjust your plan.
What could you do differently?
Could you get more information?
Get more help? Take a different approach?
Change your timing?
What have you learned from the "failure"?

Failures can hurt, of course. Think of a failure you've experienced. How did you feel about it? How did you deal with it? How do you *wish* you'd dealt with it?

◆ •••••••••••••••••••••••••••••••••••••••••••••• ◆

## The Fear of Success

**Sometimes when people pull back from serious challenges, it's not because they're afraid of failing— it's because they're afraid they'll succeed.**

Does that sound crazy? Maybe it is, but it happens—a lot. All of us, at points in our lives, have allowed ourselves to be held back by chatter in our minds that says we're not good enough—chatter that creates constraints we're scared to move past. "I'm not old enough." "I don't speak well enough." "I'm too shy." "I don't have the time or the experience or the money to do this." "Someone else could do this better than I could."

We're all tempted to listen to this stuff, especially when we're facing new challenges—whether the doubts make sense or not. Sensible or nonsense, they actually make us *comfortable* because they help us duck responsibility for helping solve the problems we see.

But when you *do* act on an issue that's meaningful to you, taking the responsibility and the risks that come with the job, when you stay active in the community of service—you find a personal power and clarity that you may never have felt before, that many people *never* feel. This affirmation of your own competence *forces* you to give up that old comfortable picture of yourself with all those limitations you thought you had. Because you know you *can*, you can no longer tell yourself you *can't*.

Turning off the chatter, giving up your perceived limitations and moving into the unknown is exhilarating. It can also make you feel vulnerable and scared, because it means taking on more responsibility than you may have bargained for, and it means accepting your own worthiness and your own ability to make a difference in your world.

Giving up your old perceptions about yourself and sticking your neck out for the common good means using everything you've got and everything you *are* to live the meaningful life we talked about at the beginning of this book.

**Don't back away from letting your life**

**be as important as it needs to be—**

**as full of meaning, vision and joy as you can make it.**

**There are many of us on this journey.**

**Thank you for letting me join you on this part of it.**

✔ Stop right now and celebrate the completion of your project.

✔ In carrying out a personal commitment to the common good, you've joined a community of people who care, and who act on their caring. You're a full-fledged, contributing member of the human family.

✔ Reflect on how your project went and on what you've learned.

✔ Consider your next project. What else needs to be done?

✔ Whatever the issue might be, the guidance in this book becomes even more relevant as projects get bigger.

✔ If and when you suffer a setback, use it to learn something, rather than as a reason for giving up.

✔ Fear of success comes from hanging on to that old comfortable picture of yourself with all those limitations you thought you had. Erasing that picture means accepting your own worthiness, and your ability to make a difference in your world.

✔ You *can* lead a meaningful, joyful life.

**And a few last words from the Giraffe Project Quote Bank ~**

*Service is the rent you pay for room on this earth.*
—former Congresswoman Shirley Chisholm

*The noblest question in the world is, "What good may I do in it?"*
—Benjamin Franklin

*Just to be alive and to be of service to somebody is a reward.*
—Giraffe Jo Ann Cayce

*The price of hating other human beings is loving oneself less.*
—Eldrige Cleaver

*How wonderful it is that nobody need wait a single moment before starting to improve the world.*            —Anne Frank

*Example is not the main thing in influencing others. It is the only thing.*
—Albert Schweitzer

*If we don't start growing people who will commit themselves to causes beyond their personal pocketbook, we're in such deep trouble—global warming doesn't even come close to creating the crisis that you have in a country where there's no community ... where it is not accepted as part of the fabric of the community that you contribute.*—Giraffe Maria Varela

*You may be disappointed if you fail, but you're doomed if you don't try.*
—Beverly Sills

*Everybody can be great because everybody can serve.*
—Martin Luther King, Jr.

# RESOURCES

The following pages give you many of the groups, books, videos and Websites the Giraffe Project finds useful and interesting. Look here for ideas, tips, leads, inspiration, information—there's a world of good stuff going on, and the door to the part you're looking for may be on these pages. In your search, don't overlook the tried and true places that are *not* listed here. Faith-based organizations, community centers, and youth groups such as 4H and Scouting, all have service opportunities you can pursue.

# Organizations

Entries marked by a ⚑ were founded by and/or are led by people who have been commended as Giraffes by the Giraffe Project.

## Categories of organizations

Community Development
Community Service
Diversity
Entrepreneurship
Environment
Homelessness

Human Rights
Hunger
Media Activism
Substance Abuse Prevention
Violence & Crime Prevention

## COMMUNITY DEVELOPMENT

### ⚑ ⚑ Habitat for Humanity

121 Habitat Street
Americus GA 31709-3498
912-924-6935 or 1-800-HABITAT

A grassroots organization that helps low-income families build their own homes. Founded in 1968 by Giraffes Linda and Millard Fuller, its goal is to completely eliminate poverty housing and homelessness by connecting families in need with people of all ages who have the resources or time to help. Send for information about chapters in your area and how to get involved, a newsletter, and a catalog of gifts made from around the world—proceeds help build more homes.

*Website: http://www.habitat.org*
This site gives the history of HFH, facts on housing and homelessness, news of current projects, and information on how to get involved. You can also email questions to publicinfo@habitat.org.

### OXFAM America

26 West Street
Boston MA 02111-1206

This international organization works in partnership with the poor, giving them access to the basic resources necessary to move out of poverty. OXFAM's educational outreach includes hunger awareness programs such as "Hosting a Hunger Banquet," and information on hunger, fasting and fundraising.

*Website: http://www.oneworld.org/oxfam/*
More information on OXFAM and its current projects. The site also has press releases, catalogs, and current information on international issues of concern.

**Peace Corps**
1111 20th Street NW
Washington DC 20526
1-800-424-8580
Peace Corps Volunteers travel overseas and make real differences in the lives of real people. PCVs teach children the basics of math, science, and English; work with communities to protect the local environment; help people stay healthy, expand their businesses, grow more nutritious food—the jobs and the locations are all over the map. Get details online.
*Website: http://www.peacecorps.gov/*

## COMMUNITY SERVICE

### Center for Living Democracy
RR#1 Black Fox Road
Brattleboro VT 05301
802-254-1234 Fax 802-254-1227
The Center focuses national attention on democratic breakthroughs so that they become the new standard by which people measure their progress. The Center helps citizens learn from each other's triumphs and setbacks. They offer a catalog of useful materials.
*Website http://www.livingdemocracy.org/*

### Constitutional Rights Foundation
601 South Kingsley Drive
Los Angeles CA 90005
213-487-5590
The Foundation's interest is in making the Constitution and the Bill of Rights come alive in young people's lives. To help kids become active in the community, CRF offers mini-grants for student-planned service-learning projects.
*Website: http://www.crf-usa.org*

### DO Something
423 West 55th St, 8th floor
New York NY 10019
212-523-1175
The goal of this group is to inspire young people to believe that change is possible, and to train, fund and mobilize them to be leaders who strengthen their communities. They offer national grants to people under 30 for creative community-based projects.
*Website: http://www.dosomething.org/*

### The Giraffe Project
PO Box 759 197 Second Street
Langley WA 98260
360-221-7989 Fax 360-221-7817
email: office@giraffe.org
The nonprofit that created this book, as part of the Giraffe Heroes Program.
*Website: http://www.giraffe.org*
Online stories, articles, information, quotes, links and products.

### National Youth Leadership Council

1910 West County Road B
St Paul MN 53113
651-631-3672 Fax 651-631-2955
email: nylcusa@aol.com

NYLC's quarterly, *The Generator,* is packed with service-learning ideas, programs, field reports, and new ideas for the implementation of technology and service in the classroom. NYLC also hosts annual conferences for educators of all grade levels and interests.

*Website: www.nylc.org*

### Youthwish Foundation

128 Riviera Drive
Tavernier FL 33070

Youthwish was established by Giraffe Ellen Bigger to encourage fellow young people to build and sustain their own community service projects. Youthwish provides small matching grants for student-generated service projects. Write for an application.

### City Year

285 Columbus Avenue
Boston MA 02116
617-927-2500

City Year unites young adults across boundaries of race, class, age, gender, education, and geography, as City Year corps members who put their talents and ideas to work tutoring and mentoring children in local schools, creating afterschool and vacation programs, teaching violence prevention and HIV/AIDS awareness, revitalizing parks and gardens, and participating in community initiatives.

*Website: http://www.cityyear.org*

## DIVERSITY

### Anti-Defamation League

823 United Nations Plaza
New York NY 10017
212-490-2525

One of the country's largest distributors of human relations audiovisuals and print materials.

*Website: http://www.adl.org/*

### National Women's History Project

7738 Bell Road
Windsor CA 95492
707-838-6000

Giraffes Mary Ruthsdotter and Molly Murphy MacGregor co-founded the NWHP and initiated the celebration of National Women's History Month. Their mail order catalog offers multicultural books, posters, videos, and classroom materials about women's history.

*Website: www.nwhp.org*

**Teaching Tolerance**
400 Washington Avenue
Montgomery AL 36104
334-241-0726 ext. 374

Giraffes Morris Dees and Joseph Levin founded the Southern Poverty Law Center, which publishes a curriculum that fosters interracial and intercultural understanding, and a semi-annual magazine with ready-to-use ideas and strategies. Teachers can get a free curriculum package by having their principal send a written request, or the magazine by sending their own request, on school letterhead.

*Website: http://www.splcenter.org*

**UNITY: United National Indian Tribal Youth, Inc.**
PO Box 25042
Oklahoma City OK 73125
405-424-3010

This organization offers a newsletter and youth leadership training, and an annual national Native American Youth Leadership Conference.

## ENTREPRENEURSHIP

**Fund for Social Entrepreneurs**
1101 15th St NW Suite 200
Washington DC 20005
202-296-2992

A project of Youth Service America, this fund hosts a contest for national and community service ventures. Winners get a two-year stipend and a $4,000 seed grant for their project.

**Junior Achievement**
www.ja.org

Junior Achievement's offices are all over the country; you can find the nearest one on their website, which also describes their programs, scholarships and history, going back to 1919!

**National Foundation for Teaching Entrepreneurship**
120 Wall Street, 29th floor
New York NY 10005

This nonprofit organization, founded by Giraffe Steve Mariotti, contracts with schools to teach kids of all ages how to start and run businesses. NFTE has an array of materials on the subject, including the BIZBAG, a young entrepreneur's start-up kit.

*Website: http://www.aybc.org/rescenter/progserv/nfte.html*

**Youth Venture**
1700 North Moore Street Suite 1920
Arlington VA 22209
703-527-8300 ext. 223

Youth Venture is building a mass movement of young people who are launching and running their own ventures. They help young people find adult allies and funding in their communities.

*Website: http://www.youthventure.org*

## ENVIRONMENT

**Captain Planet Foundation**
One CNN Center, South Tower, 10th floor
Atlanta GA 30303
404-827-4130

This foundation gives grants of $250 to $2,500 for environmental projects. Unfortunately kids can't apply themselves; a teacher must do the application. Some parameters: the projects must be hands-on activities that take kids out of the classroom; they should reach a large number of students or be expandable to such an outreach; and preference is given to urban and rural schools. Write for guidelines.

*Web: http://www.turner.com/cpf/*

**Center for Environmental Education**
Antioch New England Graduate School
40 Avon Street
Keene NH 03431-3516
310-454-4585

A resource center for students and teachers. Their newsletter, *Grapevine*, includes center news, the latest in research, fundraising ideas, information about other environmental organizations, book lists, and an events calendar.

**Pachamama Alliance**
PO Box 29191
San Francisco CA 94129-9191
415-561-4522 Fax 415-561-4521
info@pachamama.org

Pachamama works with indigenous peoples to stop the destruction of their cultures and of the rainforests. Their materials on living sustainably in our own culture are excellent.

*Website: http://www.pachamama.org/*

**Rainforest Action Network**
221 Pine Street Suite 500
San Francisco CA 94104
415-398-4404 Fax 415-398-2732

Information on how to help stop the destruction of the rainforests, including the addresses and phone numbers of relevant politicians and businesspeople to contact. Ask for "Seven Things You Can Do to Save the Rainforest."

*Website: http://www.ran.org*

### Roots & Shoots
The Jane Goodall Institute
PO Box 599
Ridgefield CT 06877
203-431-2099  Fax: 203-431-4387

An environmental awareness organization that has grown out of Goodall's realization that saving wildlife, such as the gorilla community she has so long studied, depends on saving habitat in the largest possible way. Newsletters, information kits, and connections to a growing network of concerned activists.

*Website: http://www.janegoodall.org/rs/rs_history.html*

### Student Environmental Action Coalition
PO Box 31909
Philadelphia PA 19104-4711
215-222-4711

A student-run organization of over 1,500 high school and college environmental groups sharing resources and building coalitions through conferences, newsletters and trainings.

*Website: http://www.seac.org*

### The World Wildlife Fund
1250 Twenty-fourth Street NW
Washington DC 20037-1175
202-293-4800

One of the oldest and largest environmental organizations in the world, WWF uses legislation, education, boycotts and publications to preserve and guard the fragile diversity of our planet. WWF not only assists countries to stop the poaching and exploitation of endangered creatures and habitat, it also educates people about alternatives to destroying the ecosystem. WWF has many materials for educators.

*Website: http://www.panda.org/*

Most of the available information from WWF is online. Look here for a photo gallery, slide show, age-appropriate texts and information, fact sheets, news clippings, global alerts, information on how to get involved, and links to other environmental pages. The site is available in several languages.

### ▌ Youth for Environmental Sanity (YES!)
420 Bronco Road
Soquel CA 95073-9510
877- 293-7226

Founded in 1990 by 16-year-old Ocean Robbins and 19-year-old Ryan Eliason, this group offers inspirational presentations nationally to high schools and colleges. They host two- and three-week-long summer camps in seven countries that inform, inspire and empower youth ages 15-25 to take positive action for healthy people and a healthy planet. YES!'s World Youth Leadership Camp brings together outstanding young environmental leaders from 20 countries for a week of networking, skills sharing, and community building.

*Website: http://www.yesworld.org*

# HOMELESSNESS

### Christmas In April
1536 Sixteenth Street NW
Washington DC 20036-1402
202-483-9083

Taken national by Giraffe Patricia Riley Johnson, CIA is a nonprofit that rehabs the homes of the elderly or disabled. Volunteers work in over 150 affiliated community projects across the country. CIA can send you information about participating, donating, or forming your own group.

### Happy Helpers for the Homeless
403A Old Stage Road
Glen Burnie MD 21061

When she was 8, Giraffe Amber Coffman organized her friends to distribute bag lunches to the homeless in her area once a week. Over the years, she's recruited volunteers and solicited food from bakeries, grocery stores, orchards, and local businesses. Amber has a starter kit for kids who are interested in helping their communities' homeless.

### National Coalition for the Homeless
1012 Fourteenth Street NW #600
Washington DC 20005-3410
202-737-6444 Fax 202-737-6445

Founded by Giraffe Chris Sprowal, NCH is committed to ending homelessness. Twenty percent of the board of directors are homeless or formerly homeless men and women, with an insider perspective on just how to help solve the problem.

*Website: http://www.nch.ari.net*

Information about the crisis of homelessness, including current facts and legislation, stories from homeless families and children, information on how to join the coalition, and links to other organizations working to abolish homelessness.

# HUMAN RIGHTS

### Amnesty International
322 Eighth Avenue
New York NY 10001
212-807-8400 or 800-266-3789

AI watchdogs international human rights violations. Students can sign on to write letters asking for fair and humane treatment of political prisoners. AI publishes a catalog of educational materials and resources for promoting human rights awareness and action. Also available though the catalog are AI's reports on countries' activities and special books, videos and CD-rom interactive programs.

*Website: http://www.amnesty.org*

This site provides information in several languages about human rights violations, current events and issues, Amnesty's global activities, news releases, and links with other organizations.

# HUNGER

### Heifer Project International
Overlook Farm
216 Wachusett Street
Rutland MA 01543
508-886-2221

This group takes a self-help approach to world hunger and poverty, helping families and communities in need worldwide to produce food and income for the long-term. Their education materials address the root causes of hunger and poverty. You can write, call or check the Website for information about their programs, school visitations and field trips.

*Website: http://www.heifer.org*

### The Hunger Project
15 East 26th Street
New York NY 10010
212-251-9100 Fax 212-532-9785

This group works to end hunger by providing basic structures to help people help themselves. They also provide materials for classes interested in addressing hunger as a project, information on starting service-oriented clubs, and a monthly report.

*Website: http://www.thp.org*

Students and teachers can access basic information about the Project, international anti-hunger activities, texts and articles from the UNICEF conference on hunger, and more.

### The Potato Project
3383 Sweet Hollow Road
Big Island VA 24526
800-333-4597

When Giraffes Ken Horne and Ray Buchanan learned that America wasted 20 percent of its annual potato crop, they started the Potato Project. The group now distributes healthy but commercially "unacceptable" potatoes and other produce to soup kitchens, disaster victims, food banks, and shelters in 48 states. They can tell you how to contribute time or money, or how to bring The Potato Project to your area.

*Website: http://www.endhunger.org/grficpg1.htm*

### Results
440 First Street NW #450
Washington DC 20001
202-783-7100 Fax 202-783-2818

Giraffe Sam Daley-Harris founded Results to rally the political will to end hunger. Results has been called "Pound-for-pound, the most effective lobbying group in Washington DC." The group puts out alerts when legislation on hunger is pending, and has good background information on hunger issues and actions in this country and worldwide.

*Website: http://action.org*

### Rock and Wrap it Up

405 Oceanpoint Avenue
Cedarhurst NY 11516
516-295-3848

It seems that there's a lot of good food backstage at rock concerts and that most of it isn't eaten. Rock and Wrap it Up collects it all and gets it to hungry people. They have information on how students can start similar endeavors with surplus cafeteria food.

*Website: http://www.rockandwrapitup.org*

### Second Harvest

116 South Michigan Avenue Suite 4
Chicago IL 60603-6001
312-263-2303 or 800-532-FOOD

This is a national network of 181 food banks and the largest hunger relief organization in the US, distributing food and grocery items to over 50,000 charitable agencies that serve more than 26 million people each year. They can give you information about the organization, its efforts, and how to get involved.

*Website: http://www.secondharvestsjca.org*

Second Harvest Food banks in Santa Clara and San Mateo Counties in California have gone online. Look here for statistics, how to sponsor a food drive, more information about Second Harvest and instructions for donating to Second Harvest.

### Trees For Life

3006 West St. Louis
Wichita KS 67203
316-945-6929 Fax 316-945-0909

Giraffe Balbir Mathur founded this organization to fight hunger by planting food-bearing trees. Trees For Life has planted two million such trees in the US, India and Brazil, helping people become self-sufficient. TFL has planting programs and how-to kits for individuals and for classes. Kids can also raise money to buy trees that TFL will distribute.

### World Hunger Year

505 Eighth Avenue 21$^{st}$ floor
New York NY 10018-6582
212-629-8850 Fax 212-465-9274

WHY serves as the National Hunger Clearinghouse, providing information on over 3,000 organizations in all 50 states. They have presentations, publications, and a curriculum for students.

*Website: http://www.iglou.com/why/htm.*

This site presents valuable information about the organization, and about getting started in your own community, plus quizzes, facts, background, a list of the 100 most significant books about hunger, links to other hunger and poverty pages, press releases and membership information.

# MEDIA ACTIVISM

### Activist's Web Starter Kit
Cyberspace is a great place to organize, strategize and rally people who are working on the same issues. Check out this site for advice on creating your own website.
*Website: http://www.2.portal.ca/~comprev/webkit.htm*

### Center for Media Literacy
4727 Wilshire Boulevard Suite 403
Los Angeles CA 90010
213-931-4177
The Center for Media Literacy provides leadership, training and a direct mail clearinghouse of books, videos and teaching materials for schools, churches, afterschool programs, parent groups and community centers. Issues covered include kids and television, media and politics, sexism/racism in media and tobacco/alcohol advertising.
*Website: http://www.medialit.org*

### FAIR (Fairness and Accuracy In Reporting)
130 West 25th Street
New York NY 10001
212-633-6700
FAIR is a national media watchdog group working to correct bias and imbalance in the depiction of women, minorities, working people, and other public interest constituencies.
*Website: http://www.fair.org/fair/*

### The Media Foundation
1243 West 7th Ave
Vancouver BC CANADA V6H 1B7
This nonprofit publishes *Adbusters* magazine, an often hilarious, always clever send-up of the advertising world.
*Website: http://www.adbusters.org*

### Mediascope
12711 Ventura Boulevard
Studio City CA 91604
818-508-2080
Mediascope promotes constructive depictions of health and social issues in film, video games and music, and on TV and the Internet, particularly as they relate to young people.
*Website: http://www.mediascope.org*

### TV-Free America
1611 Connecticut Avenue NW Suite 3A
Washington DC 20009
202-887-0436
This group encourages Americans to reduce the amount of television we watch so we can lead richer, healthier and more productive lives. They sponsor National TV Turn-off Week every April.
*Website: http://www.essential.org/orgs/tvfa*

## SUBSTANCE ABUSE PREVENTION

### The Badvertising Institute
PO Box 8052
Portland ME 04104
Giraffe Bonnie Vierthaler, a professional artist, has created what she calls "badvertise-ments" that tell the truth about tobacco use. An exhibit of the ads has toured all 50 states and is now available on slides and as wall posters.
*Website: http://www.badvertising.org*

### Center on Alcohol Advertising
2140 Shattuck Avenue Suite 1206
Berkeley CA 94704
510-649-8942
This organization works with national and regional groups, legislators, community leaders and the public, promoting public policy changes that stop the advertising of alcohol to kids.
*Website: http://www.pcvp.org/alcohol/*

### National Center for Tobacco Free Kids
1707 L Street NW Suite 800
Washington DC 20036
202-296-5469 or 800-284-KIDS
This group is raising awareness that tobacco use is a pediatric disease, and changing public policies to prohibit the marketing of tobacco to kids.
*Website http://www.tobaccofreekids.org*

## VIOLENCE & CRIME PREVENTION

### Center to Prevent Handgun Violence
1225 Eye Street NW Suite 1100
Washington DC 20005
202-898-0792
The Center educates the public about gun violence and has been at the forefront of the movement to reform the gun industry's sales and marketing practices.
*Website: http://www.handguncontrol.org*

### Center for the Study and Prevention of Violence
Institute of Behavioral Science/
University of Colorado at Boulder
Campus Box 442
Boulder CO 80309-0442
303-492-8465
CSPV collects and distributes research on the causes and prevention of violence, offers tech-nical assistance for the evaluation and development of violence prevention programs, and researches the causes of violence and the effectiveness of prevention and intervention pro-grams.
*Website: http://www.colorado.edu/cspv*

**◪ Save Our Sons And Daughters (SOSAD)**
2441 West Grand Boulevard
Detroit MI 48208
313-361-5200

Founded by Giraffe Clementine Barfield after she lost her son to random street violence, SOSAD runs a Survival Institute that helps kids move away from violence and gangs, teaches conflict resolution in Detroit schools and operates a community garden. They can send you information about gangs and street violence and the location of the SOSAD chapter nearest you.

**Stop the Violence...Face the Music Society**
723 Casino Center Blvd  2nd floor
Las Vegas NV 89101-6716
800-732-6366

STV acts to counter youth violence via nonviolent, anti-crime, anti-drug messages in music, videos and literature.
*Website: http://www.stv.net*

# BOOKS OF INTEREST

Babbie, Earl, *You Can Make a Difference*, Opening Books. 1985
A thoughtful and thought-provoking book providing both inspiration and guidance for people of all ages who want to make a difference.  Many stories of people already putting their heroic potential to work.

Berger, John J., *Restoring the Earth*, Anchor Press/Doubleday, 1987
Thirteen inspiring success stories of environmentalists, including Giraffe Marion Stoddart, who launched the cleanup of the Nashua River.

Berkowitz, Bill, *Local Heroes*, Lexington Press, 1987
Stories of ordinary people accomplishing extraordinary things; many of them are Giraffes.

Campbell, Joseph, *The Hero With a Thousand Faces*, Mythos:Princeton/Bollingen Series in World Mythology, revised 1990
The writer who tutored George Lucas on heroic myth-making during the creation of *Star Wars*. Campbell was and remains the ultimate authority on the archetype of the hero.

Coles, Robert, *The Call of Service: A Witness to Idealism*, Houghton Mifflin, 1993
A look at what inspires people to serve their communities, and what sustains them over time.

Cosgrave, Gary & Pat Kery, *Stop, Think and Dream: Be the difference that makes a difference*, IONS, 1999
A collection of winning poster designs created by New York City teenagers addressing the question, "What kind of planet do we want to live on?"

Daloz, Keen, Keen and Parks, *Common Fire: Lives of Commitment in a Complex World*, Beacon Press, 1996
Stories and analysis of the lives of more than a hundred people in many walks of life who live and work for the common good. Practical recommendations for individuals, families, businesses, educators—anyone interested in a life of meaning.

Fiffer, Steve and Sharon, *50 Ways to Help Your Community*, Doubleday, 1994
A good resource for class discussion, ideas for projects, and easy-to-follow steps for positive change.

Ford, Clyde W., *The Hero With an African Face: Mythic Wisdom of Traditional Africa*, Bantam Books, 1999
Ford fills in a missing piece of Joseph Campbell's work in heroic mythology—the hero stories of the African continent. Also by Ford:
> *We Can All Get Along*, Dell, 1994
> 50 steps to ending racism. Included are suggestions for eliminating prejudice and stereotypical thinking.

Gerzon, Mark, *A Choice of Heroes: The Changing Face of American Manhood*, Replica Books, 1999
Always an interesting thinker, Gerzon looks at the stereotypes of male heroism and proposes new ideas on what men's lives are about.

Goleman, Daniel, *Emotional Intelligence: Why It Can Matter More Than IQ for Character, Health, and Lifelong Achievement*, Bantam Books, 1995
Drawing on groundbreaking brain and behavioral research, Goleman maps out the territory of what constitutes emotional intelligence and shows how being "emotionally smart" may be more important to the individual and to society than being intellectually bright.

Graham, John, *Outdoor Leadership: Technique, Common Sense and Self-Confidence*, The Mountaineers, 1997
By the author of the book you're holding, *Outdoor Leadership* covers many of the issues in *It's Up to Us*, using outdoor situations as the context. All of its stories and ideas apply equally well to life indoors and in cities.

Grier, Rosey, *All-American Heroes*, MasterMedia, 1993
The former football great shares the histories and successes of multicultural Americans of all ages. Upbeat and inspirational, each story includes a quote worth hanging onto.

Harris, Sam, *Reclaiming Our Democracy: Healing the Break Between People and Government*, Camino Books, 1993
Harris (now Sam Daley-Harris), Giraffe and founder of Results, gets to the heart of what it means to be an active citizen in a democracy. Inspiring, informative and exciting.

Hoose, Philip, *It's Our World, Too*, Little Brown, 1993
Stories of young people who are making a difference by taking on challenges they see in their communities and beyond. Many of them are Giraffes.

Josephson, Michael & Wes Hanson, ***The Power of Character***, Jossey-Bass, 1998
Prominent Americans, including The Giraffe Project's Ann Medlock, share their observations on living with integrity, honesty and compassion in today's world.

Lewis, Barbara A., ***The Kids Guide To Social Action***, Free Spirit Publishing, 1991
Addressed to middle and high school students, includes ideas for creative thinking, positive change, and helpful tips for getting started.

Loeb, Paul Rogat, ***Soul of a Citizen: Living with Conviction in a Cynical Time***, St. Martin's, 1999
A look at active citizens, what they're accomplishing, and the importance of active citizenship in a healthy democracy.

Robbins, Ocean, and Sol Solomon, ***Choices for Our Future***, Book Publishing Company, 1994
Writing to assist teen environmentalists, Giraffe Ocean Robbins and his co-author explain how the choices we all make factor into saving the planet.

Seo, Danny, ***Generation React: Activism for Beginners***, Ballantine Books, 1997
A blueprint for a cleaner, healthier world via concerned activism, filled with practical suggestions to help anyone, from Giraffe Danny Seo, founder of Earth 2000.
Also by Seo:
> ***Heaven On Earth:15-Minute Miracles to Change the World***, Pocket Books, 1999
> Suggestions for ways to benefit your community in just 15 minutes a day.

Seligman, Martin E.P., ***Learned Optimism***, Pocket Books/Simon & Schuster, 1990
Fascinating account by a psychologist of how we can move out of self-defeating pessimism by understanding the ways we explain life to ourselves—and changing those ways.

Waldman Jackie with Janis Leibs Dworkis, ***The Courage to Give***, Conari Press, 1999
Accounts of people who have persevered beyond their own pain to help others. Includes chapters by Giraffes Bo Lozoff, Brianne Schwantes, Millard Fuller, Bill Thomas, Jeff Moyer, Giraffe Project President Ann Medlock, and an afterword by Giraffe Patch Adams.
Also by Waldman:
> ***Teens with the Courage to Give***, Conari Press, 2000
> Profiles and photos of 30 teens who have moved out of personal trauma and into service, including Giraffes Jason Crowe and Michael Munds.

Wuthnow, Robert, ***Learning to Care: Elementary Kindness in an Age of Indifference***, Oxford University, 1995
Stories of young people involved in community service.

# VIDEOS AND WEBSITES

### Connect
Distributed by Magic Baby
PO Box 23363
Seattle WA 98102
email: connect@magicbaby.com

Chosen to air internationally as MTV's 1997 Earth Day Special. this 23-minute video is hosted by Michael Stipe of R.E.M., and is filled with environmental images from around the world and with young activists speaking boldly about making a difference for the earth.

### The Culture Jammer's Video
Distributed by The Media Foundation
1243 West 7th Avenue
Vancouver BC CANADA
*Website: http://www.adbusters.org*

This definitive media literacy tool contains some of the best social marketing campaigns ever produced. Suitable for everything from classroom viewing to neighborhood discussions. 14 minutes.

### In The Mix
Distributed by PBS.
*Website: http://www.pbs.org/wnet/mix*

A youth-oriented TV news magazine series that focuses on issues of interest and concern to today's teens. Typical of the series: Tyra Banks and Bill Novelli cohost a half-hour special, "Smoking: The Truth Unfiltered."

### www.oneworld.org

A great site for current issues, news and altruistic projects worldwide. If you're looking to get involved or just looking for information, this must-see site gives you media clippings and pictures from over 80 countries, environmental information, education resources, and links to other service-minded organizations with Websites.